HOW TO GET WHAT YOU WANT

ORISON SWETT MARDEN

2015 by McAllister Editions (MCALLISTEREDITIONS@GMAIL.COM). This book is a classic, and a product of its time. It does not reflect the same views on race, gender, sexuality, ethnicity, and interpersonal relations as it would if it was written today.

CONTENTS

1 SOMETHING TOUCHED HIM 1
2 HOW TO GET WHAT YOU WANT 12
3 PLAYING THE GLAD GAME 30
4 DISCOURAGEMENT, A DISEASE HOW TO CURE IT 42
5 THE FORCE THAT MOVES MOUNTAINS 55
6 FAITH AND DRUGS 73
7 HOW TO FIND ONESELF 88
8 HOW TO ATTRACT PROSPERITY 101
9 THINKING ALL OVER 116
10 HEART-TO-HEART TALKS WITH YOURSELF 133
11 OUR PARTNERSHIP WITH GOD 149

1
SOMETHING TOUCHED HIM

THE MOST valuable thing whichever comes into a life is that experience, that book, that sermon, that person, that incident, that emergency, that accident, that catastrophe – that something which touches the springs of a person's inner nature and flings open the doors of their great within, revealing its hidden resources.

A cub lion, as the fable runs, was one day playing alone in the forest while his mother slept. As the different objects attracted his attention, the cub thought he would explore a bit and see what the great world beyond his home was like. Before he realized it, he had wandered so far that he could not find his way back. He was lost.

Very much frightened, the cub ran frantically in every direction calling piteously for his mother, but no mother responded. Weary with his wanderings, he did not know what to do, when a sheep, whose offspring had been taken from her, hearing his pitiful cries, made friends with the lost cub, and adopted him.

The sheep became very fond of her foundling, which in a short while grew so much larger than herself that at times she was almost afraid of it. Often, too, she would detect a strange, far-off look in its eyes which she could not understand.

The foster mother and her adopted lived very happily together, until one day a magnificent lion appeared, sharply outlined against the sky, on the top of an opposite hill. He shook his tawny mane and uttered a terrific roar, which echoed through the hills. The sheep mother stood trembling, paralyzed with fear. But the moment this strange sound reached his ears, the lion cub listened as though spellbound, and a strange feeling which he had never before experienced surged through his being until he was all a-quiver.

The lion's roar had touched a chord in his nature that had never before been touched. It aroused a new force within him which he had never felt before. New desires, a strange new consciousness of power possessed him. A new nature stirred in him, and instinctively, without a thought of what he was doing, he answered the lion's call with a corresponding roar.

Trembling with mingled fear, surprise and bewilderment at the new powers aroused within him, the awakened animal gave his foster mother a pathetic glance, and then, with a tremendous leap, started toward the lion on the hill.

The lost lion had found himself. Up to this he had gamboled around his sheep mother just as though he were a lamb developing into a sheep, never dreaming he could do anything that his companions could not do, or that he had any more strength than the ordinary sheep. He never imagined that there was within him a power which would strike terror to the beasts of the jungle. He simply thought he was a sheep, and would run at the sight of a dog and tremble at the howl of a wolf. Now he was amazed to see the dogs, the wolves, and other animals which formerly had so terrified him flee from him.

As long as this lion thought he was a sheep, he was as timid and retiring as a sheep; he had only a sheep's strength and a sheep's courage, and by no possibility could he have exerted the strength of a lion. If such a thing had been suggested to him he would have said, "How could I exert the strength of a lion? I am only a sheep, and just like other sheep. I cannot do what they cannot do." But when the lion was aroused in him, instantly he became a new creature, king of the forest, with no rivals save the tiger and the panther. This discovery doubled, trebled and quadrupled his conscious power, a power which it would not have been possible for him to exert a minute before he had heard the lion's roar.

But for the roar of the lion on the distant hill, which had aroused the sleeping lion within him, he would have continued living the life of a sheep and perhaps would never have known that there was a lion in him. The roar of the lion had not added anything to his strength, had not put new power into him; it had merely aroused in him what was already there, simply revealed to him the power he already possessed. Never again, after such a startling discovery, could this young animal be satisfied to live a sheep's life. A lion's life, a lion's liberty, a lion's power, the jungle thereafter for him.

There is in every normal human being a sleeping lion. It is just a question of arousing it, just a question of something happening that will awaken us, stir the depths of our being, and arouse the sleeping power within us.

Just as the young lion, after it had once discovered that it was a lion would never again be satisfied to live the life of a sheep, when we discover that we are more than mere clay, when we at last become conscious that we are more than human, that we are gods in the making, we shall never again be satisfied to live the life of common clods of earth. We shall feel a new sense of power welling up within us, a power which we never before dreamed we possessed, and never be quite the same again, never again be content with low-flying ideals, with a cheap success. Ever after we will aspire. We will look up; struggle up and on to higher and ever higher planes.

Phillips Brooks used to say that after a man has once discovered that he has been living but a half-life the other half will haunt him until he releases it, and he never again will be content to live a half-life. When one becomes conscious that the reality of them, that the truth of their being is God, that they are indissolubly connected with omnipotent power, they feel the thrill of divine force surging through every atom of their being, and can never doubt their divinity or possibilities again. They can never again be timid, weak, hesitating or fearful. They rest serenely conscious that they are in close touch, in vital union, with the Infinite. They feel omnipotent power pulsating through their very being, they feel the omnipotent arm sustaining, upholding them, and they know that their mission on earth is divinely planned and divinely protected.

Many a poor child has grown up in the slums believing that they were like all the other children in their neighborhood, that there was no special future for them, nothing distinctive, nothing out of the dead level of their monotonous environment; but something unexpectedly happens, some emergency, some catastrophe, something which makes a tremendous call upon the great within of themselves, and they are suddenly surprised to discover that they are different altogether from those about them. Something has touched them, something in them have been aroused, something which shows them that they have a tremendous latent power which they did not before know they possessed, and they unhesitatingly answer the call. They go out into the great world, and are never again satisfied with a cheap success, never again satisfied with their old nature or content with their old environment.

There are men and women who have won distinction in every field who would not believe that there was such a possibility for them until they had actually proved it. Twenty-five years ago, for instance, you could not have persuaded Charles M. Schwab that he was the man later years have proved him to be. If twenty-five years ago anyone had given a picture of himself as he is today, had declared that he would be such a man, he would have ridiculed the idea. He would have said, "Such a thing is absurd, I am not such a man. This is the picture of a giant. I am no giant, nor genius. I am just an ordinary, hard-working man." But Mr. Schwab has not even yet fully found himself. He has not discovered all the man that it is possible to develop, or anything like it. He has only brought out part of the giant in him. Emergency may sometime call out the rest, the bigger giant.

There are plenty of young men and young women in our great industrial institutions today who could not be made to believe that perhaps in a single year they will be filling positions of great responsibility and power, and yet the possibility is there. The future great general, the successful executive, is slumbering in the soldier in the ranks, in the clerk today. Many a future superintendent, many a manager is today filling the humble position of office boy, errand boy, or waiter in a restaurant or hotel.

Every discovery of new powers, new assets in yourself, stimulates you tremendously to new efforts, to new endeavor. We have all seen instances where an ordinary clerk, with seemingly ordinary ability, has suddenly been promoted, and the stimulus, the tonic of advancement, the new hope of further success that has prodded them, has often added twenty-five or fifty per cent to their ability by uncovering new resources, new and before undreamed of powers.

They were not conscious of what was in them until the opportunity came, until the motive uncovered, unlocked and liberated their before undreamed of resources. In the last world war thousands of young men who did not think they had much courage, perhaps even believed they would be cowards in battle, were whirled into the armies by the excitement, the hypnotism, the daring of their associates, and found that the bigger man in them responded to the call, and that when it came they did not hesitate bravely to face the enemy's shells, the enemy's guns. Many youths have joined the army who were not thought much of at home, who were called stupid and dull and ne'er-do-wells, blockheads, by their parents and teachers, but when they got into the army they found themselves, found they had courage, grit, determination, daring, stick-toit-iveness.

The experience of a multitude of men who have realized an infinitely bigger man in themselves than they ever imagined was there, ought to teach us that in every human being, no matter how successful they may be, there are still enormous undiscovered possibilities.

It is the person you are capable of making, not the one you have become, that is most important to you. You cannot afford to carry this enormous asset to your grave unused. As a business man or woman you would not think of having a lot of idle capital in the bank, drawing no interest, uninvested, unused. Do you realize that this is exactly what you are doing with yourself? You have assets within you infinitely more valuable than money capital. Why do you not use your capital? This is what you would ask a businessman who was pinching along, worried all the time because he thought he could not meet his obligations, pay his notes, when he had a large amount of idle capital in the bank. You would declare the man was foolish. You are more foolish because you have immortal capital lying idle. Why don't you use it? Why do you hitch along in this little one-horse way all your life on a little capital when you have so much unused capital, so much reserve assets? Why not use them?

Try to bring out that possible man or woman. You know that you never have done it to anything like its possibility as yet. Now, why not plan to bring out this enormous residue, these great unused resources, this locked-up ability which has never come out of you? You know it is there. You instinctively feel it. Your intuition, your instinct, your ambition tell you that there is a much bigger person in you than you have ever found or used. Why don't you use them, why don't you get at them, why don't you call them out, why don't you stir them up? Why don't you get the spark to this giant powder within you and explode it?

The finding of the larger possibilities of man, the unused part, and the undiscovered part is the function of the New Philosophy. It may be covered under all sorts of debris – doubt, lack of self-confidence, timidity, fear, worry, uncertainty, anxiety, hatred, jealousy, revenge, envy, selfishness. These may all be neutralized by right thinking.

How often it happens that people who have long been "down-and out," who have been considered "nobodies," "good-for-nothings," not well balanced, have changed suddenly, as though touched by a magic wand, and have quickly become men or women of power, inspirers, and helpers of others! Something happened that quickened their spirit, and from miserable liabilities they have suddenly been converted into valuable assets to their community.

John B. Gough was an intemperate nobody. All at once, apparently by accident, he was converted. Something touched Gough and from being a slave of the bottle he became its master. From a miserable example he was transformed into a tremendous uplifting and inspiring force in the community. Before he came to himself he was dragging men down; after he responded to the call of the divinity within, he was leading hundreds and thousands of men to take the pledge, to lead cleaner and nobler lives.

When a poor youth working as scullion in a kitchen in Italy first got a glimpse of a great painting, the sight aroused something within him which he had never before felt. It revealed a new artistic impulse, and he exclaimed, "I, too, am a painter!" Following this inward call, he got a chance to work in the studio of a famous artist, and finally became a greater artist than the painter of the picture which had inspired him.

How many men who had been a positive menace to society, all at once have turned about and become inspired leaders! Something touched them, awakened the God within, and they turned their faces from darkness to light, from the lower to the higher, and accomplished grand things. It may have been an inspiring book, a lecture, or a flash of divine illumination that gave them a glimpse of themselves, but whatever it was it started them on the right road, turned them from ugliness to beauty, from wrong to right, from enemies of society to great benefactors.

The transformation of Saul the persecutor into Paul the great apostle of the Gentiles is one of the grandest instances of self-revelation through a flash of divine illumination.

What a revolution would be effected in the whole race if this something which touched Saul on his way to Damascus, when "suddenly there shined round about him a light from heaven," could touch all the human beings who are going wrong, the "nobodies," the "down-and-outs," the discouraged, the despondent, those who have fallen by the wayside! What a leap toward the millennium the race would take if all these dead souls could be awakened and made anew by this mysterious something which made the vengeful persecutor of Christians the greatest of the teachers of Christianity! If this divine spark, which enkindles a new fire in human hearts, makes men out of beasts, and good citizens out of hoboes, drunkards and criminals, could be ignited in the breasts of all, despair and misery would vanish from the earth.

When one has once discovered or uncovered a bit of their divine pattern, when enough light is thrown upon it to enable them to see the divine, immortal plan foreshadowed in their nature, they will never be content until they uncover the rest of the pattern; and no one can do this by living a coarse, low, sensual life. Such a life puts a film on the ideals, and dims the spiritual vision.

The world has a right to expect those who have even partly discovered themselves, who have become conscious of their divine origin, to hold up their heads, to do their work a little better, to be a little more dead-inearnest, to live on a higher plane, to set a little better example in general than those who have not yet tasted of their hidden power. The world needs great inspirers more than it needs great lawyers, physicians, clergymen or statesmen. It needs the Lincolns more than it needs railroad magnates, steel magnates, great financiers or great merchants.

When the consciousness of his heredity touched the lion cub, when

his inheritance of strength, of terrific power, was revealed to him, he turned his back forever on the old life. Never again could he return to the sheepfold, never again could he be satisfied with his sheep nature, with the half-life he had been living. From the moment he realized he was a lion, there was no more sheepfold for him. Freedom, the great open world, the jungle, the forest for him, for he felt his kingship, his power over all the things that had so terrified him in the past.

When an individual has once proved beyond question that they have great latent power, vast possibilities which had never before been called out, it would be impossible that they should ever again be satisfied with the half-life they had been living. Their whole newly discovered nature would revolt against a return to the lower plane on which their weaker, lesser self had lived.

You perhaps were reared under conditions which have kept you ignorant of your own possibilities until something has happened to throw a new light upon your real nature. Then you discovered that you were not the tame, timid sheep that you had always thought you were, until that something happened which has revealed the lion in you.

Perhaps you have been wandering all your past life, living in the shepherd's folds in the churches, perhaps never dreaming that you were not a sheep, that you did not belong to that particular shepherd's fold. Yet you may have had an instinctive feeling that there was something in you which did not respond to the sheep call, that there was a something within you which did not fit your environment, which did not belong to the conditions in which you found yourself. You may have been conscious that there was something in you which never responded to the call which appealed to those about you.

You may have heard the voice that answered your yearning while reading an inspiring book, or while listening to a new philosophy conversation which seemed to open up a new compartment in your nature.

No matter where you hear this call, when you do hear it something within you will answer the call and you will know that you have been touched to a higher, a finer purpose.

The new philosophy, however, especially appeals to the undiscovered part of us, to those hidden, latent forces within us, which we have not hitherto been able to get hold of. In other words, it appeals to our hitherto unused assets, our plus or surplus life capital. You will find something in people who have embraced it, in people who understand it, which you do not find in others.

The new philosophy acts like a leaven in the nature, giving new life, new force, new meaning to the individual. In short, it discovers a new human being in the old one. It neutralizes, destroys, that which would degrade them, those things which were working against their welfare, and it develops new forces, unlocks new resources which enlarge the individual.

During the past hundred years not a single new quality or new principle has been added to the laws of chemistry, not an iota of change has been made in the laws of physics, and yet what miracles of discovery, of invention, the great scientists and inventors have called out of these very same qualities and laws during the last hundred years!

Sir Isaac Newton had the same identical material, the same identical laws of chemistry, physics which Edison is using today, but Edison has called out hundreds of inventions to Newton's one discovery.

Human nature, like natural law, is the same today as it was centuries ago, but what a marvelous development of man's power we are witnessing today! How amazing has been the advancement of human ability! What marvelous strides in intelligence, in efficiency, and in the development of his natural resources man has made!

We marvel at all this, but the new philosophy is disclosing to man a new and more potent law back of the flesh but not of it, an intelligence back of the crystal, back of the atom, back of the electron which directs, molds, fashions, conditions the future of every particle of matter in the universe. Previously this was ascribed to an unknown law. A hundred years ago people did not know that when a crystal was dissolved it would always assume the exact form of the same kind of crystal when its particles were free to rearrange themselves. We did not then know that the ambition which appears in man is really an aggregate of the ambition in the separate electrons. We did not then know that a man's history was largely determined in the electrons themselves. But science is now beginning to recognize that the great cosmic intelligence is back of everything in the universe, of every expression of nature, of every step in man's upward journey through the ages.

The new philosophy especially appeals to that unknown part of us which is still waiting to be discovered, that part which is still locked up tight in the great within of us. It plays the part of a Columbus, and discovers vast territory within us of which we had been unconscious.

An honest dissatisfaction with our achievement means we have more resources inside, and that until we find at least a measure of satisfaction there is still more to discover. We have an instinctive feeling, that there is something sublimely beautiful in life we have never yet found, because we have never yet been satisfied. We have an intuition that this something will satisfy our inmost yearnings, that it will quench the soul's thirst, satisfy the soul's hunger.

The orthodox churches undertook to find this satisfying something, and while they have done much, yet many church members feel that there is still a tremendous, unfilled vacuum in their hearts, unsatisfied longings and yearnings in their souls. After centuries of hunting for the divine balm of Gilead, the elixir which would heal the soul's hurts, the great majority of churches are being less and less frequented. Pastors are finding it more and more difficult to induce people to attend their church services, because they are not fed; they do not get that satisfaction which they instinctively feel belongs to the children of the King of Kings.

On every hand we find people who have been groping all their lives in vain, trying to find something which would answer the inner call for a larger life, something which would satisfy their longings, feed their soul hunger, and help them to find fulfillment of their life dreams.

If you are groping to find that something which will give enduring satisfaction, which will satisfy your soul; if you have not yet found that something which answers the persistent inward call of your being; if you have not yet found that living water which quenches the soul's thirst, come and drink at the fountain of the new philosophy.

Man has glimpsed only a little bit of the divine plan, but this glimpse promises so much that he feels he must see the whole. The part of ourselves we have discovered reveals only a part of the divine pattern, and we shall never rest until we trace the whole.

The larger, grander, superb thing we know and instinctively feel we ought to be beats so mightily so persistently beneath the little dwarfed thing we are that we must uncover it, we must develop it, and we must use it. No human being can be satisfied while they are haunted by that other part of the divine pattern, the part which was shown to them in the mount of their highest moment. The part of ourselves we have discovered is a prophecy of an infinitely larger and more magnificent whole, and we must find it. This is the great object of our existence. We are here to find the rest of the pattern of the divine man.

Individually we have gotten a glimpse of the larger possible man, and we must bring them out. We have been shown a part which prophesies the possible whole, and every now and then lest we become discouraged and give up the pursuit, nature gives us a Lincoln, a Gladstone, a Phillips

Brooks, in order apparently to show us the possibilities of man and to stimulate us in our efforts to evolve the God man.

The new life philosophy is the Christ motive which has been working in man all up through the ages in its efforts to produce the master man, not the selfish, grasping, greedy man, but the masterful, selfless, impersonal man, the Christ like man or woman with the God consciousness, the man or woman who realizes that they are part of all mankind; that they have come out from God and that they are going back to God.

2
HOW TO GET WHAT YOU WANT

YOU ARE victory organized; you were born to conquer, to play a magnificent part in life's great game. But you can never do anything great or grand until you have such a conviction of yourself and your ability.

We establish relations with our desires, with whatever is dominant in our minds, with the things we long for with all our hearts, and we tend to realize these things in proportion to the persistency and intensity of our longings and our intelligent efforts to realize them.

Stop thinking trouble if you want to attract its opposite; stop thinking poverty if you wish to attract plenty. Refuse to have anything to do with the things you fear, the things you do not want.

A piece of magnetized steel will attract only the products of iron ore. It has no affinity for wood, copper, rubber, or any other substance that has not iron in it. When you were a boy you found that your little steel magnet would pick up a needle but not a match or a toothpick. It would draw to itself only that like itself.

Men and women are human magnets. Just as a steel magnet drawn through a pile of rubbish will pull out only the things which have an affinity for it, so we are constantly drawing to us, establishing relations with, the things and the people that respond to our thoughts and ideals. Our environment, our associates, our general condition are the result of our mental attraction. These things have come to us on the physical plane because we have concentrated upon them, have related ourselves to them mentally; they are our affinities, and will remain with us as long as the affinity for them continues to exist in our minds.

Your thoughts, your viewpoints, your conception of what your status and position in life will be, your ideal of your future, will draw you exactly to that plane like a lodestone. Focus your mind, your predictions, your expectations on poverty, failure and wretchedness; banish ambition, hope, expectation of good things, and give full sway in your mentality to fear, worry, doubt, anticipation of evil, and the ego magnet will draw you unerringly to squalid surroundings, to an inferior position, to association with persons of a lower order of mind on a meaner social plane.

The great trouble with all of us who are struggling with unhappy or unfortunate conditions is that we have separated ourselves in some way from the great magnetic center of creation. We are not thinking right, and so we are not attracting the right things. "Think the things you want." The profoundest philosophy is locked up in these few words. Think of them clearly, persistently, concentrating upon them with all the force and might of your mind, and struggle toward them with all your energy. This is the way to make yourself a magnet for the things you want. But the moment you begin to doubt, to worry, to fear, you demagnetize yourself, and the things you desire flee from you. You drive them away by your mental attitude. They cannot come near you while you are deliberately separating yourself from them. You are going in one direction, and the things you want are going in the opposite direction.

"A desire in the heart for anything," says H. Emilie Caddy, "is God's sure promise sent beforehand to indicate that it is yours already in the limitless realm of supply."

No matter how discouraging your present outlook, how apparently unpromising your future, cling to your desire and you will realize it. Picture the ideal conditions, visualize the success, which you long to attain; imagine yourself already in the position you are ambitious to reach. Do not acknowledge limitations, do not allow any other suggestion to lodge in your mind than the success you long for, the conditions you aspire to. Picture your desires as actually realized, and hold fast to your vision with all the tenacity you can muster. This is the way out of your difficulties; this is the way to open the door ahead of you to the place higher up, to better and brighter conditions.

When Clifton Crawford, the actor, started on his career in America, he played in one-week performances in small towns and cities. One night he was told by a prominent member of the company that his work wasn't much good, that he would never be successful, and had better go back home to Scotland. Notwithstanding this discouraging but well-meant criticism and advice, young Crawford remained in America, continued in his profession and in a comparatively short time reached the coveted position of a Broadway "star." After his first success in New York he had the satisfaction of meeting the friend who had advised him to return to his own country, and reminded him of the incident.

Clifton Crawford won out because he related himself mentally to the thing he wanted, because he listened to the voice in his own soul rather than to the pessimistic predictions of outside voices.

Why has the heart restless yearnings
For heights and steps untrod?
Some call it the voice of longing
And others the voice of God.

That something within you which longs to be brought out, to be expressed, is the voice of God calling to you. Don't disregard it. Don't be afraid of your longings; there is divinity in them. Don't try to strangle them because you think they are much too extravagant, too Utopian. The Creator has not given you a longing to do that which you have no ability to do.

One reason why the lives of many of us are so narrow and pinched, small and common-place, is because we are afraid to fling out our desires, our longings, afraid to visualize them. We become so accustomed to putting our confidence only in things that we see on the physical plane, in the material that is real to the senses, that it is very difficult for us to realize that the capital power, the force that does things, resides in the mind. Instead of believing in our possession of the things we desire, we believe in our limitations, in our restrictions. We demagnetize ourselves by wrong thinking and lack of faith. We see only the obstacles in our path, and forget that man, working with God, is greater than any obstacle that can oppose itself to his will.

Benjamin Disraeli knew this when he said, "Man is not the creature of circumstances. Circumstances are the creatures of man." He demonstrated its truth in his own life. Alien in race and creed, with other circumstances apparently dead against him at the start, the resolute young Jew overcame all obstacles, and reached the goal of his ideal. He became Prime Minister of England, and was made Earl of Beaconsfield by his sovereign, Queen Victoria. Lowell did not utter a mere airy, poetic idea when he said, "The thing we long for, that we are, for one transcendent moment."

He spoke a simple truth. The poet is always the prophet. He goes ahead of the scientist, and points the way that leads upward to the ideal. Like faith, the poet knows and sees far in advance of the senses. He knows that the vision of our exalted moments is the model given us to make real on the material plane.

The men who have climbed up in the world have seen themselves climbing, have pictured themselves actually in the position they longed to be in. They have climbed up mentally first. They have kept a vision of themselves as ever climbing to higher and higher things. They have continually affirmed their ability to climb, to grow up to their ideal. If we ever hope to make our dreams come true, we must do as they did; we must actually live in the conscious realization of our ideal. This is the entering wedge which will split the difficulties ahead of us, which will open the doors which shut us from our own.

If you are discouraged by repeated failures and disappointments, suffering the pangs of thwarted ambition; if you are not doing the thing you long to do; if life is not yielding the satisfaction, the success and joy of happy service; if your plans do not prosper; if you are hampered by poverty and a narrow, crude, uncongenial environment, there is something wrong – not with the world, or the Creator's beneficent plans for His children, but with yourself. You are not thinking right. You are not visualizing yourself as you long to be.

We are, every one of us, both ourselves and our environment, true pictures of what we have thought, believed, and done in the past. Every moment of our lives we are experiencing the result of thought. The outward things that have been acting on us, shaping the conditions in which we live, are chiefly the fruits of our own motives, thoughts and acts. What we believe, what we think, what we expect, shapes our lives. Through the control and direction of our thoughts, backed up with corresponding efforts on the physical plane, we can attract to us all our heart's desires.

How often do we hear it said of some man, "Everything he undertakes succeeds," or "Everything he touches turns to gold?" Why? Because the man is constantly picturing to himself the success of his undertakings and he is backing up his vision by his efforts. By clinging to his vision, by vigorous resolution and persistent, determined endeavor he is continually making himself a powerful magnet to draw his own to him. Consciously or unconsciously, he is using the divine intelligence or force by the use of which every human being may mold himself and his environment according to the pattern in his mind.

Why don't you use your divine power to make yourself what you long to be? Why don't you cling to the vision of yourself which you see in your highest moment, and resolve to make the vision a reality? By persistent right thinking, backed by the steady exercise of your will, you can, if you desire, remake yourself and your environment. Since we can "for one transcendent moment" be the thing we long for, you and I and every human being can make that transcendent or highest moment permanent. It is purely a matter of right thinking. Every time we visualize the thing we long for, every time we see ourselves in imagination in the position we long to fill, we are forming a habit which will tend to make our highest moments permanent, to bring our vision out of the ideal into the actual.

If people only knew the possibilities which center in the highest development of their visualizing powers it would revolutionize their lives.

Until comparatively recent times most of the country between Omaha and the Rocky Mountains was a vast barren desert, and it looked as though it would always be absolutely worthless. Many intelligent men wondered why the Creator ever made such a dreary waste as these millions of acres presented, and when it was suggested in Congress that the Government assist in building a railroad across this desert from the

Missouri River to the Pacific Slope, even men like Webster laughed at the idea. Webster said that such an undertaking would be a wicked waste of public money, and he suggested the importation of camels for the purpose of carrying the United States mail across the Western desert. He believed this was the only use that could be made of those waste lands.

But the vision seen by the men who conceived the Union Pacific Railroad was no idle dream; it was a foreshadowing of the reality. Before a rail had been laid, these men saw great thriving cities, vast populations and millions of fertile farms springing up like magic where the men without a vision of its possibilities saw nothing but alkali plains, sage brush and coyotes. It was the men who were not limited by appearances, by what the senses told them, who transformed the desert into a thing of beauty and untold wealth.

Human beings are like this arid desert, packed with marvelous possibilities which are just waiting for that which will arouse their latent forces and make the germs of those wonderful possibilities blossom into beauty and power. What we need is a firm belief in the vision of ourselves which we see in the moment of our highest inspiration. As soon as we feel the touch of the awakening, arousing, energizing power of an unalterable faith in our own divinity, in our ability to be "the thing we long for," our lives will blossom into beauty and grandeur.

The realization of our power to create ideals and to make these live in reality is destined to revolutionize the world, because we build life through our ideals. This power to build mentally is the pathway of achievement, the way which will lead to the millennium. We cannot accomplish anything, do anything, create anything except through an ideal, a vision.

"The vision that you glorify in your mind," says James Allen, "the ideal that you enthrone in your heart – this you will build your life by, this you will become.

"The thoughtless, the ignorant, and the indolent, seeing only the apparent effects of things and not the things themselves, talk of luck, of fortune and chance. Seeing a man grow rich, they say 'How lucky he is!' Observing another become intellectual, they exclaim 'How highly favored he is!' And noting the saintly character and wide influence of another, they remark, 'How chance aids him at every turn!' They do not see the trials and failures and struggles which these men have voluntarily encountered in order to gain their experience; have no knowledge of the sacrifice they have made, of the undaunted efforts they have put forth, of the faith they have exercised, that they might overcome the apparently insurmountable, and realize the vision of their heart."

The reason why so many people fail to realize their ideals is that they are not willing to do their part to make it real. Remember that the longing, the desire to do a certain thing, is merely sowing the seed of your ambition. If you stop at this you will get about as much harvest as the farmer would get if he put his seed in the ground without preparing the soil, without fertilizing it and keeping the weeds down.

You must back up that which your heart longs to realize with an honest purpose to do your best, a dead-in-earnest effort to make your vision real. The mere holding of the desire to do so, no matter how persistently or strongly you hold it, will not help you to realize your dreams. You must not only sow the seed of desire and longing, but you must do all the nourishing, cultivating, caring for, or you will only reap a thistle harvest. We see men and women everywhere reaping a very thistly, a very weedy harvest from the sowing of mere longings. These people can scarcely get enough out of their harvest to keep them alive, simply because they took no care of their seed after the planting.

The constant nursing, cultivating the desire, the ambition, keeping our heart's longings and soul yearnings alive, wholesome and healthy by active endeavor, is the only way in which we can match our dreams with their realities.

Watch an immigrant boy who lands in America practically with nothing but the clothes he wears, without knowing our language or customs, and with no friends, no "pull" to advance him, and see how quickly he outdistances many American youths who were born and brought up in the very lap of opportunities. Why? Because this boy constantly thinks and dreams of making his way in the world. He sees himself a successful man, and is forever planning and pushing toward his object.

He begins, perhaps, by selling newspapers in the streets. Then his ambition grows and he dreams of someday having a newsstand. He attends night school in order to get an education. He toils and economizes, flings his enthusiasm and his whole being into his work, is constantly enlarging his mind and also making himself a magnet to attract the thing he longs for. He is obeying the law of attraction, of opulence, and in a little while we see him with a news stand of his own. But he does not stop here. He keeps dreaming, planning, working for something a little larger, and soon he adds books and stationery to his stock in trade. Before long we find him with a large stand in a railway station or in some public place, always saving, and dreaming, planning, thinking success. In a few years more he owns a handsome shop and becomes a real factor in the business world. His whole mental life is poured into that one channel, and of course he is perpetually increasing his magnetic power to attract to himself money and all the other things he desires.

The ambition to become rich is not a lofty one, but the success of this typical immigrant boy illustrates the law of success in every field. For the law is neither moral nor unmoral, the nature of the object concentrated on does not affect its action. It may be the noble vision of a Jeanne d'Arc, of a Savonarola, or of a Lincoln, or it may be a wholly selfish, or an unworthy object, the attractive, constructive forces will build just the same toward the realization of the vision. If a man's ambition is to own saloons and sell liquor or to be the proprietor of a gambling resort, and he keeps working away on the material as well as the mental plan, he will succeed, just as a man who works in a similar way to become a teacher, or a missionary, succeeds. The same concentration, the same absorption, the same dreaming and thinking and pushing along any other line, law, medicine, engineering, science, farming, whatever it may be, will produce like results. The idea is that the everlasting dreaming and pushing, the alertness to take advantage of opportunity, the constant visualizing of the thing one yearns for most, inevitably bring the desired results. These are the constructive processes, based on the mental vision, which bring us the things we desire.

What we think most about is constantly weaving itself into the fabric of our career, becoming a part of ourselves, increasing the power of our mental magnet to attract those things we most ardently desire.

When the architect looks at the plan of his building he does not see the plan merely. That only suggests the building. It is the invisible building, the creation of his mind he sees. What he takes in from the plan with his eyes is not the reality at all. He sees in all its details the building of his mental vision. If he did not see it in this way, it would never become a reality. If he could see only the mechanical plans he would not be an architect at all.

The framework of your life structure is invisible. It is on the mental plane. You are laying the foundation for your future, fixing its limits by the expectations you are visualizing. You cannot do anything bigger than you plan to do. The mental plans always come first. Your future building will merely be carrying out in detail what you are visualizing today. The future is simply an extension of the present. You are right now by your thought habit, by your prevailing mental attitude, making your place in life. You are locating yourself, settling what you are to be. In other words, you are right now making your future, deciding what your position in the world shall be. And it will be broad, ever growing, ever expanding, or it will become narrower, more pinched and rutty, according to your mental plan, according to the vision you see.

The only world you will ever know anything about, the only world that is true for you at this moment, is the one you create mentally – the world you are conscious of. The environment you fashion out of your thoughts, your beliefs, your ideals, your philosophy is the only one you will ever live in.

Whatever you long for you are headed toward, and whatever thought dominates you, or motive is uppermost in your mind, is attracting its affinities. How quickly, for example, a youth who goes from his country home to the city to seek his fortune gravitates toward the things which are uppermost in his mind. He may not know a soul in the city he enters, but in a very short time we find him with his own people, those whose tastes, whose desires and propensities are like his own. He has attracted his affinities.

One boy's mind is fixed on pleasure, and he gravitates to the saloon, to the dance hall, to the vicious dives, to the gambling table. Another boy's great desire is self-improvement, and he gravitates to the Y.M.C.A., to some church. We find him in the night schools, in the libraries, or attending lectures, trying to improve his education, to make as broad-visioned, as cultured and successful a man as it is possible to make of himself.

The same thing is true of girls. They gravitate toward their desires, their ideals, toward the things on which they have set their hearts. Led by their weaknesses or their strength, they are pulled in the direction on which their thoughts are fixed, whether good or bad.

If ten thousand strangers from other cities were landed in New York today and left to their own devices, they would very quickly be attracted to their affinities. The gambler would find other gamblers, the musician would gravitate to other musicians, the artist would be drawn to art circles; the pure minded, those of high ideals, would soon find others on the same plane, while the impure minded, those with vulgar, low flying ideals, would as quickly find companions like themselves.

A mental magnet cannot attract opposite qualities. It can only attract things like itself, and it is our privilege to give the magnet its quality. We can inject hate into it, jealousy, envy, revenge; we can in a very short time demagnetize the magnet which was pulling good things so that it will attract bad things. It is for us to decide the quality of the magnetic current that shall flow out from us, but the mind is always a magnet sending out and attracting something, and this something which flows back to us always corresponds to the mental outflow.

If we charge it with love, sincerity, genuineness, helpfulness, great spiritual hunger for the good, the beautiful and the true, a longing for a larger and a fuller life, we shall make the mind a powerful magnet to attract the affinities of these qualities. But in an inconceivably short time we can so completely change our mental magnet with thoughts of hatred, spite and bitterness that it will drive away all the good and attract the opposite, strengthening the hatred and bitterness in our souls.

In short, whatever is in the mind at the moment is the thing you are inviting to come and live with you. Your suspicion attracts suspicion. Jealousy brings more jealousy, hate more hate, just as love brings love to meet it, as friendliness brings more friendliness, as sympathy and good will toward all draw the same to you from others and increase your popularity and magnetic power.

We build as we think. Our lives follow our thoughts. As we think so we are. Your personality and your world are limited by the extension of your own thought. You cannot project yourself beyond these self limitations. Many people limit themselves to such an extent by their gloomy doubts and fears that they utterly dwarf their divine powers and possibilities. They do not believe that their own is coming to them. They are always complaining, visualizing their poverty-stricken conditions, their lack of friends, their lack of sympathy, their lack of love, of opportunity, of social life, of everything desirable. They do not realize that they are their own jailers, that they are holding themselves in the very conditions they despise. They have not learned how to make themselves magnets for the things they desire. They do not know that our own is seeking us and will come to us, whether it is property, friends, love, happiness, or any other legitimate desire, unless we drive it away by our antagonistic thought.

If you did not believe you had the power to walk you couldn't walk, because you wouldn't try to. If you don't believe in your power to get what you want you won't get it. Until you encourage your longings and believe in your power to realize them they will never be satisfied. You cannot rise out of your present condition until you believe you can. The limit of your thought will be the limit of your possibilities. Your limited ideal of yourself will limit your execution. You will never get any higher than your vision and your faith in that vision.

No one gets very far in this world, or expresses great power, until he catches a glimpse of his higher self – until he feels that the divinity which is stirring within him, and which impels him on the way of his ambition, in the line of his aspiration, is an indication, a prophecy of his ability to reach the ideal which haunts him. The Creator has not put desires in our hearts without giving us the ability and the opportunity for realizing them. There are a thousand proofs in the very formation of our body and brain that we were planned and adapted in every detail of our marvelous structure to achieve grand, glorious things, that we were created and fitted for success and happiness.

No matter how unfortunate your environment, or how unpromising your present condition, if you cling to your vision and keep struggling toward its realization, you are mentally building, enlarging your ideal, increasing the power of your mental magnet to attract your own.

Never mind opposition, never mind criticism, never mind if others call you a fool or a crank – they called the Christ the same – be true to the mysterious message within, the divine voice which bids you up and on. No matter what other things you have to give up, no matter what sacrifices you have to make, let everything else go if necessary, but cling to the ideal which haunts your dreams, for it points to the star of your destiny, and if you follow it you will come out of the darkness into beauty and brightness. Your highest ideal, the vision of your life work which you long to make real, is your best friend. Keep as close to it as you can, stick to it, and it will lead you to your goal. You may not understand why the star has been put so high above you and why so many mountains of obstacles and difficulties intervene, but if you keep your eye on the star and listen to the voice of your soul which bids you climb on, you will reach it.

Many a man has never been able to explain his success, or how he was able to wring it out of such a black background, such iron conditions and seemingly impossible surroundings, as those in which he found himself at the start. But he kept pegging away, never losing sight of his ideal, which became his guiding star, his success angel, which ultimately led him through the dark valleys of difficulty and opposition, up out of the miasma of the stagnant swamps of discouragement to the heights, where the atmosphere is pure, the outlook clear, where excellence dwells. It led him out of the darkness into the light, into freedom, into success.

Just because you are struggling on a farm or in a factory, doing something against which your whole nature rebels, because there is no one to help you support your aged parents or an invalid brother or sister, do not conclude that your vision must perish. Keep pushing on as best you can, and affirming your divine power to attain your desire. Hundreds and thousands of poor boys and girls with poorer opportunities than yours have done immortal deeds because they had faith in their ideal and in their power to attain it.

It is by the perpetual focusing of his thought upon the solving of scientific problems, added to his faith in his ability to solve these problems, that Edison has attracted to himself the forces which have made him the greatest living inventor. His mind has always run ahead of him, visualizing the invention he was trying to bring out into objective reality. He was always picturing himself a little higher up, a little further on, and his success has followed his vision and his faith.

Suppose Edison had lost faith in his vision; suppose he had allowed obstacles to discourage him and had said to himself, "Thousands of men have been thinking along these lines, trying to solve these problems for a long time, and have failed, and how can I expect to succeed? Why should I waste my time and energies in trying to do what they found impossible?" – do you think he would have become the power he is? Of course, he would not, – he couldn't, any more than Marshal Field could have become a great merchant if he had listened to those who tried to discourage him. Doors always open, opportunities always come, to the man or woman who trusts and works, but nothing comes to the weak, doubting heart, the faint endeavor, nothing comes to those who do not believe in their divinity, their power to overcome.

No matter how black and forbidding the way, just imagine that you are carrying a lantern which always advances with you and gives you light enough for the next step, and although it looks very dark and discouraging a little distance ahead, when you arrive there the light will arrive also. All the light you need is for the next step, to know that you are going in the right direction. In other words, you must have faith, trust. The divine plan that has created us, given us a part in the plan of the great universe, will bring things out better than we could if we will only do our part.

Look back upon your past lives, you self-made men and women, and see how miraculously the doors have opened out of the blackness ahead of you, so that you were able to enter into the Eden of your dream, to accomplish the thing you so long dreamed of!

Goodyear was a dreamer and a seer of visions long before he was able to vulcanize rubber. Morse was a "visionary" or we might not have had the telegraph. Cyrus W. Field had a wonderful vision of an ocean cable, and had he not gone on dreaming of his cable in spite of his disappointments the nations of the world might still be dependent on ships to transmit their messages from one to the other. Had Eli Whitney not been a seer of visions the black people of the South might still be picking the seeds from cotton by hand. But for the dreams of Marconi's youth, wireless telegraphy might have been postponed for a century. Had it not been for the dreams and longings of Alexander Graham Bell we might not even yet be talking over the wire. Had Elias Howe not dreamed of a sewing machine women might still be slaves of the needle.

Had it not been for Phillips' and Garrison's and Lincoln's dream of freedom, millions of our countrymen might still be in slavery.

All of these people – every inventor, every discoverer, every up-lifter of the race, all those who have lifted civilization up from the Hottentots to the Lincolns and the Gladstones, have clung to their vision in spite of incredible sufferings and obstacles. Nothing could turn them from their purpose or shake their faith in their power to make their vision a reality. This was why they won out.

Men succeed in proportion to the fixity of their vision and the invincibility of their purpose. If you can find out a man's quitting point, the place where he gives up, turns back, you can measure him pretty easily.

The man who conquers is the one who moves, steadily, persistently, everlastingly towards his goal, unmindful whether the goal is always in sight or not, unmindful of obstacles, of difficulties, of discouraging conditions. He moves ever forward, just as Columbus did when he wrote day after day in his log boat, undaunted even when his sailors mutinied, threatening to put him in chains and to throw him overboard: "This day we sailed west because it was our course." This was his daily record, because there was nothing else for him to do but to sail west. A man with such a mighty purpose as Columbus's wouldn't have turned about if his crew threatened murder every day, because he was invincible. Nothing but death could have stopped his onward course.

What could have stopped Farragut from going into Mobile Bay past the enemy's torpedoes? What could have stayed a man with such a mighty purpose, such invincible determination that he lashed himself to the mast, lest if he was shot or wounded he might fall overboard or be captured in his perilous run past the torpedoes!

Washington showed his invincibility of purpose and fixity of vision at Valley Forge as few men have ever shown it. In fact, this grim courage in face of difficulties, this fixity of vision and inflexibility of purpose have been characteristic of all the great men of history, to whom the world has built monuments.

Science tells us the eagle's wings developed in response to the eagle's desire to fly, to soar into the ether. Your longings, your yearnings for something higher and grander, your aspirations, backed by an invincible purpose, will call out your wings, will develop your latent power, so that you will rise above your mediocre environment to the full measure of your possibilities.

If all our youth were taught to keep the soul vision inviolable, never to tamper with that sacred something within which always points heavenward if left alone, that something which, no matter how poor or iron our environment, bids us look up and not down, aspire and not grovel, civilization would advance with marvelous strides towards the millennium.

The limit of your faith in your vision and in yourself is the limit of your achievement. Faith is the greatest magnetic power we know of for the attraction of the things that belong to us.

A great faith, a sublime self-confidence was the magnet which attracted to John Wanamaker that which made him a merchant prince. When young Wanamaker was delivering his first order of clothing in a pushcart in the streets of Philadelphia, he did not keep his mind fastened on his poverty and limitations, and fear he would never get past them. On the contrary, he thought of a great future, and when he went past the big rich stores he pictured himself as a great merchant, and felt confident that the time would come when he would have a bigger and richer store than any of them.

Where self-faith is weak, the will is weak. Most people do not exert their will in overcoming the obstacles in their way, because their resolutions are weak, wishy-washy. They are not possessed by their vision, and so they cannot bring to their aid the vigorous determination, the resolute will, the compelling affirmation, that wins out in spite of all opposition. They are not backed by the intense desire to realize their vision that forces one to work and to sacrifice for it.

Desire is at the bottom of every achievement. It has ever been the great molding, shaping force in civilization. Desire is prayer. Our prayer is behind and at the bottom of all our achievements.

Desire is behind all progress. Civilization rests upon it. Our cities are the representations of the desires of those who built them. Every railroad train is a bundle of desires, of inventors' discoveries, of mechanics' desires.

Our homes are manifested desires. Our libraries are made up of multitudes of desires of the authors who wrote the books. Our schools, our colleges, our universities are nothing but desires fulfilled, objectified dreams of those who have built them. Every institution rests upon desires. Our lives, our homes, our friends, are all manifested desires.

All great achievements, great discoveries and inventions began in longings and desires. The success of every poor boy and girl who have pushed to the front began in longing, in indefinite yearnings, which they had the faith and the courage to nurse and back up until they realized their dreams. There is a great difference between the yearnings of the body, the workings of bodily desires and passions, and the yearnings and longings of the soul. The soul longings are really the God urge in us, the expressions of the divinity within, of the cosmic intelligence. They open the windows of the mind and give us a glimpse of the realities that were prepared for us at the foundation of the world. They are not empty imaginings, but the substance of hoped-for things, the realities of unseen things, the precursors of the things themselves.

We are apt to think that what we do in the world, our life work, is purely a personal choice. But there is something inside of us, if we are honest and earnest, that is leading us toward our own, the thing we were made to do. The youth answers an advertisement, "Boy Wanted," and gets a place which does not at all fit him, but the divine urge within haunts him until he changes. Again and again he may be a round peg in a square hole, but this inner urge – call it ambition, aspiration, a divine leading, what you will – keeps at him until he find his own, the place that fits him.

We cannot believe that Abraham Lincoln found the White House by accident or by following a selfish personal ambition. No, he was led by the Spirit to the great work for which he was born, and for which all his previous experience had been molding him.

And this same divine urge which led Lincoln out of the forest to the White House is active in every human being. There is a divine messenger detailed at every birth to follow the individual through life. This divine messenger acts as guide, is always pointing out the right road and cautioning against the wrong. If we follow the divine promptings, we shall come to our own. The poor boys who have shaped American history never dreamed when they left the farm in the backwoods, or the little village in which they were born, that they were destined to do great things. They simply followed their instinctive leadings without thinking much about, or really recognizing, their divine origin.

The mysterious unrest in the great within of us, which is ever urging us on, is an expression of the divine principle inherent in every atom, in every electron in the universe; it is the God urge which is lifting everything up to a higher and ever higher plane. Everything in the universe is on the way to its highest possible expression, on the way to perfection, on the way to its God.

We are here to do our part in raising mankind to a higher plane by giving expression to our highest ideal, by doing the best we are capable of doing. In St. John we read: "To this end was I born, and for this cause came I into the world, that I should bear witness unto the truth." Most people do not seem to think that they came into the world for any special purpose or that they are under any obligation to bear witness to the truth. They do not seem to realize that they are bound to deliver the message entrusted to them at birth, to realize the vision shown them in their highest moment. Many act as if they were sent here to catch and grab everything they can get hold of for themselves; that they are under no special obligation to anybody but their own families. In other words, few people realize that they came into the world with any particular purpose other than to gratify their own desires, to reap the harvest that others have sown without rendering anything in return.

They regard the world upon which the open their eyes as a legitimate field, a sort of hunting ground for their own personal gratification, where they are welcome to whatever they can bag without cost to themselves. They have no appreciation whatever of the fact that billions of people who have lived in all the past have really been preparing the world for them; that they are the heirs of all who have gone before them, and that they are in honor bound to do their share in contributing to the inheritance of those who shall come after them. We of today have inherited the results of other people's efforts. We are enjoying all the inventions, all the discoveries, all the luxuries that are the fruits of the struggles and trials, the sufferings, poverty and hardship of the inventors, the discoverers, the achievers who labored to improve the conditions of mankind. We were sent here to carry their work a step farther by bringing into the actual the vision of our most divine inspiration.

The way to do this is to follow our inspiration, what our soul longs to do. You are always gravitating toward the vision you hold in mind. You will never make headway in any other direction than toward your dominant thought, your dominant desire, and your dominant motive. Visualization will sometime be found to be one of the great secrets of character building and achievement. Effort follows visualization as achievement follows effort. Jesus achieved His Christ-hood. It was not thrust upon Him. He achieved it just as we must achieve our ideal if we ever attain it. The Savior was not born a Christ. This was a result of His efforts and His work to realize His vision.

Nor did Christ hold up any inexplicable ideal for His followers when he said, "Ye too are sons of God." This had never been said before. But again and again the Savior assured His followers that the things which He had done, and even greater things, those who came after Him would do.

All through His teaching Christ assured men of their divinity. When He said, "I and my father are one," He did not refer to the fact of His own superiority, to the fact that He was more divine than others. He was always trying to convince His disciples that they could do what He did, that they were as divine as He was, and that the reason they did not perform what seemed to them miracles was their lack of faith in their divinity.

We rise with our vision. All elevation, all progress, is first mental. It is based on faith in a visualized ideal. Everything starts with a vision, and the result always corresponds to the nature of the vision and our faithfulness to it. Buddha became what he did because he gravitated towards his vision. George Washington concentrated upon a vision of liberty and a grand democracy which would be a model for the whole world, and he never ceased to struggle until the vision became a reality. Andrew Carnegie became the great iron master because he gravitated towards his vision; because of his struggles to realize that dominant vision. John Wanamaker is what he is because he concentrated upon his vision, by always reaching out toward it, always striving to match with reality his dream of a mammoth business.

Every man becomes like his ideal, realizes the vision which dominates his life, and towards which he constantly struggles.

3
PLAYING THE GLAD GAME

I AM not fighting my fight, I am singing my Song.

Life should be one glad sweet song instead of a dirge as it is with so many people. It was intended that life should be a glory and not a grind.

The new philosophy teaches that everybody ought to be happier than the happiest of us are now. Our lives were intended to be infinitely richer, grander, and more glorious than they are.

Have you ever experienced that moment which you would like to last forever? I believe the time will come when your habitual state of happiness and of satisfaction will be greater than the happiest, gladdest moment you have ever experienced.

In an article in the Atlantic Monthly entitled "Twenty Minutes of Reality," the writer described an experience he had while convalescing in a hospital after a surgical operation. It was a gray March day, with a cloudy sky. There was nothing unusually exciting or exhilarating in the convalescent's immediate atmosphere or environment, when suddenly he felt as if he had been translated to a new world of light, happiness and joy.

"I cannot say what the mysterious change was," he said. "I saw no new thing, but I saw all the usual things in a miraculous new light – in what I believe is their true light. I saw for the first time how wildly beautiful and joyous beyond all words of mine to describe, is the whole of life. Every human being moving across that porch, every sparrow that flew, every branch tossing in the wind, was caught in and was a part of the whole mad ecstasy of loveliness, of joy, of importance, of intoxication, of life . . . For those glorified moments I was in love with every living thing before me – the trees in the wind, the little birds flying, the nurses, the interns, the people who came and went. There was nothing that was alive that was not a miracle. Just to be alive was in itself a miracle. My very soul flowed out of me in a great joy."

If it is possible to live in a world of happiness and beauty for twenty minutes, is it not possible to prolong the time – to live always in such a world?

We are all seeking this enchanted world, but most of us in the same way that the little boy in the story sought it.

A poor little boy, so runs this old story, once lived in a little weatherworn cottage on the top of a hill. He was a dreamy boy and every evening at sunset he would sit on the doorstep looking down toward the valley, fascinated by a beautiful house with wonderful golden windows shining a long way off at the far end of the valley.

He was greatly dissatisfied with the poverty of his surroundings, and the sight of the house in the valley, where he had never been, made him very unhappy. "Ah," he would sigh, "what a poor miserable home my hut is! If I could only live in that beautiful house with the golden windows how happy I should be!"

One evening when the golden windows, more wonderful than ever, seemed beckoning him to come, the boy made up his mind he would go and visit the house beautiful. So, early next morning he started out. The road was dusty and the sun was hot, but the little traveler trudged on and on. At length, toward sundown he found himself at the far side of the valley. But what had become of the beautiful house he had seen from his hill-top? What he stood looking at was only an old tumble-down barn. And the wonderful windows? Alas, they were not gold at all, but just ordinary glass, and dirty and broken, too.

Tired and thirsty, the little boy flung himself on the ground with his back to the deserted barn, and sobbed bitterly. Then, slowly raising his head and looking up across the valley, through blinding tears, he saw a shining blur, – his own little cottage on the hill-top! And lo, its windows, in the light of the setting sun, were a sheet of blazing gold!

How like this little boy we grown-ups are! It is always the house in the distance that beckons. The beauty and glory of life, to our discontented, longing eyes, are always afar off in some other place and time, somewhere else than just where we are and in what we are doing. Some day we hope to enter the house beautiful, but not today. We expect that in the future, through some magic or other, through money or what money can purchase, we are going to find happiness. But no human being has ever grasped the beautiful mirage which beckons him in the distance.

Most of the people I know impress me as being greatly disappointed with what life has given them. They have not found any such future as they anticipated. When they reached those years which youth had pictured so free from care and anxiety, so satisfying to their aspirations, they found existence very ordinary, very tame, very commonplace, and far from happy. The mirage which from a distance appeared so beautiful had receded when they reached the spot from which it had beckoned, and it was still beckoning from an ever receding beyond.

The chief cause of our discontent and unhappiness is that hardly anyone is satisfied with what he has. The little simple things don't count for anything with us. We are always looking for some big thing to make us happy, – a fortune, some grand opportunity, and some indefinite happiness which we are at a loss to describe. And we seem to think that whatever this thing is that is going to make us really happy is always somewhere in the shadowy future.

"It is the tormented spirit of man that always strives to bend the universe to his desires," says Dr. Frank Crane. "Hence most souls do not fit. They are at everlasting war with fate. They do not understand how to be happy with what is, because they are always straining for what is not." Some people don't even know what they are straining for. How many of the discontented people you have ever met could give you any intelligent idea of the cause of their unhappiness? They know they are discontented, unhappy; many of them chase the world over, trying to discover something which is not discoverable, which is only a byproduct of a worthy deed; and this by-product cannot be obtained until the deed is performed.

We push and elbow our way through life and frantically struggle to get hold of things which we believe will make us happy, – and behold, the moment we grasp them, the charm, with which our imagination had invested them, vanishes!

The thing we had set our heart on and which we got into our possession yesterday is not the same thing today. It does not begin to give the pleasure which it promised, and we are no nearer satisfaction than before. But our attention is quickly attracted to something else, which we feel sure will compensate for our disappointment, and we grasp at it only to repeat the same experience – disappointment, disillusion. It does not fill the void in our hearts.

There is ever an unsatisfied longing which we spend our lives trying to fill. No matter what we may obtain in the way of material things, while we may get a certain sort of pleasure and comfort from them, they do not satisfy the inward soul hunger. They are like the different things which we take on a hot day, instead of pure cold water, to quench our thirst. We think if we could only get some soda-water, some ice cream, iced tea or coffee it would satisfy our longing, but it does not. Nothing but pure cold water will give the satisfaction we crave. All substitutes for this simplest and most plentiful of all beverages lack something. They leave us unsatisfied, with a longing for the genuine article.

Happiness is like water. There is no substitute that will take its place.

One of the strangest things in life is the false ideas everywhere prevalent regarding the nature of happiness. The general belief seems to be that it is founded on things that can be bought with money. The more money the more things, and the more things the more enjoyment, the greater the degree of happiness. But money has never yet been known to buy happiness. No one has ever yet found happiness by chasing it over the earth. It is not in our food, it is not in our drink, it is not in our clothes or material possessions; it is not in excitement or a constant round of pleasure. Happiness is born of right living. It is the child of right thinking, and right acting, of helpful service. A selfish life never knows real happiness. Greed and envy never touch it.

Half the unhappiness in the world is caused by losing the blessings which would result from the enjoyment of what we have in envying others and longing for what they have.

I know of a man and his family who a few years ago were quite content in their little cottage in the country. By some venture, however, they happened to make a few thousand dollars without working hard for it, and immediately a new longing sprang up in their hearts for a life of ease and pleasure.

Immediately these people began to dress more expensively and to struggle to get into the society of wealthy people, to climb socially. They strained in every way to keep up appearances beyond their means. Envy and jealousy of those who were better off filled their hearts. The result was that in a short time the old-time peace and harmony of the family life were entirely destroyed. The father's business affairs became involved by the strain to put his children on the same plane with those of larger means; debts piled up; everything they had was mortgaged, until even their home was in danger, and was finally lost.

When the inevitable crash came it was found that the mother, in her effort to marry her daughters into families above them, had run up big bills at dressmakers', milliners', and florists', and there was nothing left with which to save the home, which was utterly wrecked.

"Half the world is on the wrong scent in the pursuit of happiness," said Henry Drummond. "They think it consists in having and getting and in being served by others. It consists in giving and in serving others."

Happiness is something which is released from our acts, and from our thoughts. A little of it here and a little there is released from our good deeds, our unselfish service, from our right acts and thoughts. Some of it is released every time we help or encourage another soul. A little of it is released when we give a helping hand to those who have fallen under their burdens. A little of it is released from the sacrifices we make for the advantage of others.

We get our happiness just as the bee gets honey. The bee does not find honey ready-made. It must work hard for all it gathers. It can only obtain a little from each flower it visits. We do not get happiness ready-made. We sip it from the flowers of life, and, like the bee, we must get a little happiness honey here and a little there as we go through the garden of life. It is those who do most of the deeds which release happiness, and get the largest aggregate of them in their lives, who enjoy the most and are the happiest.

Every noble deed, every unselfish act, every bit of helpfulness to others, every good service to humanity, every lofty aspiration and helpful thought, good honest hard work which we love, inevitably brings an amount of happiness which corresponds with the unselfishness and the good intentions of the act.

Happiness is not a monopoly. No one can "corner" it. It is for sale in the market place of life for every one who is willing to pay the price, and that is one which all can pay.

The great mass of people does not extract ten per cent of the happiness possible in their everyday life, largely because they were never trained to think of the normal sources of enjoyment. Their minds are blank, except for the little grooves which their daily routine has stamped in their brain tissue. They are as ignorant of their possible mental resources as the early Indians were of the natural resources of this continent, when the Puritans landed at Plymouth Rock.

Ruskin said he was not so much surprised at what we suffer as at what we lose, which might furnish infinite pleasure and satisfaction. We hear a great deal about the enormous loss of our natural resources, the coal, the water power, and the forests, – but they are nothing compared to the loss in the possible resources of happiness all around us.

The things which really make life worth living are very common, and within the reach of all. How often we hear the poor berating the rich whom they envy, bemoaning the cruel fate that has kept about everything worthwhile away from them, but when we stop to take stock of life in the things that are really worthwhile, that count for most, we are pretty nearly all on equal footing.

The great Chemist himself has mixed the atmosphere so that it is just adapted to create health, vigor, robustness of body and thought and exultant feeling for all alike. The sunlight, with its marvelous chemistry, performs millions of miracles every moment in root and rootlet, in plant and flower, in tree, in animal life, in human life, while painting pictures of glorious colorings, in flower, in plant, in landscape. It has an inspiring effect, too, a beneficent influence on all life; it makes all nature rejoice, and it warms the soul of man. "I never look at a sunrise that it does not give me a sunrise feeling," says John Wanamaker. And this glorious sun is a free gift to all men.

So is time. The poorest, the humblest person on earth has the same amount of precious time as the proudest monarch or the greatest money king. Andrew Carnegie said he would give ten million dollars to have his life prolonged ten years; but all his wealth cannot purchase an instant of time. Nor has money power to purchase the best things of life, love, friendship, sympathy. The sweetest, the most desirable things we know are purchasable only with effort, with right conduct, right thought, right effort.

Lincoln said that "folks are usually about as happy as they make up their minds to be." The experience of the writer of "Twenty Minutes of Reality," as well as that of thousands of others that might be cited, shows that the possibilities of happiness are not in things or in the possession of them; that happiness is not outside of us, but inside.

Everywhere people are hunting the world over for what is really in themselves, because everything is tinted, modified, shaped by what we bring to it by our mentality. If we bring beauty to it, we find that it is beautiful. If we bring an ugly mental attitude to it, it is ugly and disappointing. The source of all happiness is inside the individual. The beauty we see in nature and the beauty we feel in music are inside of us. We all know how all nature, the very landscape, seems to laugh with us when we rejoice, seems to exult with us when we are glad, and the very sun and the flowers seem to reflect our joy.

The world is a whispering gallery which sends back the echo of our own voice. It is a mirror which reflects the face that looks in it. If we laugh, it laughs back; if we frown, it reflects a frown.

Happiness is the reaction of our mental attitude and our acts upon others. It is what they fling back to us that makes us happy or miserable. The door between us and Heaven or happiness cannot be open when the door between us and our fellow men is closed.

Right thinking means right action. If we would only hold the right thought, the constructive thought, the happy thought, the joy thought, the helpful thought, the unselfish thought each day, we should all soon become supremely happy, because, finally, happiness is a mental state. Your degree of happiness or misery today is merely a resultant of your thought. If such a large part of our days were not filled with discordant thoughts, worry thoughts, fear thoughts, envy, jealousy, hatred thoughts, perhaps half unconsciously much of the time, we would be happy instead of miserable.

"Seek ye first the kingdom of God and His righteousness; and all these things shall be added unto you." When we realize the kingdom of God or heaven, that is, the kingdom of harmony, we are in a position to attract everything else that is desirable. Christ meant that when we have put ourselves into harmony with the great Source of supply, when we have become conscious of our oneness with the One, in other words, when we reach the cosmic consciousness, we are right in the midst of the all supply.

One would think that after all these centuries of searching for happiness it would have been found by the great mass of human beings, but how few have yet found it! We have not found it because we have not understood the perfect truth of Christ's philosophy, "The kingdom of God is within you."

All through history man has been hunting for this kingdom of God outside of himself. Multitudes have thought that wealth would furnish the key to this kingdom, which would supply all of his wants. He has looked for this marvelous paradise everywhere but the right place, – within himself.

Divinely fathered and mothered by his Maker, placed in an earthly paradise, infinitely more beautiful, more glorious than any human imagination could conceive, made lord over a world filled with everything necessary to make human beings ideally happy and ideally successful, yet, after centuries of race evolution, centuries of groping after ideal conditions, centuries of searching for his highest good, man is still dissatisfied. The average man is a god playing the fool. He is still looking for happiness outside of himself.

If we had found the kingdom of heaven within, our faces would be so lighted up that we would give the impression to everybody we met that we had just come into possession of some great good fortune, something that had made us exquisitely happy.

You know how pleased people appear when they have come into possession of that which they have struggled for all their lives, people who have perhaps been poor and tried hard to get on, but who barely managed to make a living, and have suddenly fallen heirs to a fortune. How changed the appearance of the whole family! There is an unwonted light in their eyes. Hope has taken the place of despair. Buoyancy and gayety have taken the place of heaviness and gloom. In other words, they have all at once become new creatures. The light of happiness shines through their flesh, looks out of their eyes.

This is how we should all impress one another. Instead of looking miserable and forlorn, God's children ought to look as though they were supremely happy. Their physical eyes should reflect an entrancing beauty which their inward eyes should behold. Through their faces should shine that inner vision which the soul should sense. If we had found the kingdom of heaven within us the countenance of every human being would reflect a superb satisfaction, a harmony, a blessedness which only very few mortals have ever yet reflected.

It is possible for everyone to have that harmonious spirit which finds serenity and true happiness in the life he is living daily, through the resources of his own soul. The new philosophy is not that of happiness postponed to a future life, but happiness to be realized here and now – not a far away personal immortality, but immortality in an increasingly happier humanity.

One of the most unfortunate things that ever happened to the race was the teaching of the doctrine that heaven is not to be enjoyed on earth, that it is something way beyond, and that we must die to reach it.

The whole teaching of the theologians looked towards the life beyond, the life to come, every desirable thing was in the future. The present was not anything like as important to them as the future. Man was simply passing through a very disagreeable probationary state which was to decide his future for all eternity. Life was a very serious matter to them, and religion was still more serious.

The theologians of the past never dreamed that happiness is one of the great essentials of living; one that plays a tremendous part in health, efficiency and general normality. Many of them thought that the tendency to play was an indication of satanic tendencies which were subversive of religion. They didn't think man had any right in this probationary period of his existence to spend precious time in playing. It never seemed to occur to them that the suppression of the play instinct develops abnormal tendencies which often lead to insanity and degeneracy.

Practically all of the Puritans suffered from the curse of fear, which darkened all their lives. The majority of them did not know what real happiness meant. Their faces wore an anxious and sad expression. There was little or no joy in their lives because their natural love of humor and fun was constantly suppressed.

Think of the effect on a sensitive mind of the belief that an infant which had not been baptized, though it had never come to the years of understanding, did not know how to reason, and knew nothing about religion, could be punished forever and ever, and that hell was paved with infants' skulls! It was such a horrible doctrine to inject into the child nature that it seems unthinkable such a thing could be possible.

For centuries the clergy were constantly cautioning men and women against the play instinct, reminding them that it was the food of evil forces. A long, sober, sad face was regarded as a sign of piety. People who laughed and played much, who enjoyed having a good time, were believed to be on the road to destruction, and were often told that the devil was after them.

There was a great deal of the sad and morose in the old theology. Think of men living in unventilated cloisters, breathing impure air, living in an absolutely abnormal way, almost entirely secluded from human society, and suppressing completely their normal instincts, writing theology, making creeds for the great throbbing mass of humanity! These men were in no condition to produce anything that was normal for they were not normal themselves. Christ did not seclude himself, he lived in the open, mingled with the common people, was one with them. What he taught was natural, was wholesome. But what a monk in a cloister, shut out from the world, apart from active life, not in touch at all with the mass of his fellow creatures, could produce under such conditions could not be anything but sad, morose, abnormal, not at all suited to people who were living normally.

The saddest note in human life has been the theological note, and nothing has been so distorted, so garbled, and so botched as the theologians' idea of man's relation to his God.

The Creator made man for a normal life of work and enjoyment, made him to be gloriously happy. He made him to be whole, strong, and ideally perfect. Any deviation from God's plan is man's fault.

Did you ever stop to think how many times the sacred writers told us to be glad, to rejoice always? In "Pollyanna" the play which for months held immense audiences in New York spellbound, Pollyanna, that child of gladness, says: "If God took the trouble to tell us eight hundred times to be glad and rejoice, He must want us to do it – some."

"Rejoice evermore." "Let the heart of them rejoice that seek the Lord," "The joy of the Lord is your strength." "Rejoice in the Lord always; again I say rejoice." "And your joy no man shall take from you." "And your joy shall be full."

Again and again these and similar expressions are repeated all through the Bible. We are not only told to rejoice and be glad, but "to rejoice and be exceeding glad." Surely God must have meant it – some. Struggles, disappointments, difficulties, are not meant to make us sad, but to make us strong – for if we don't whine and complain, we shall be given strength to overcome all these.

When I hear people grumbling and complaining about trifles and magnifying molehills into mountains, I always think of an old lady whose life had been full of sorrows and disappointments, but who never lost her cheerfulness and serenity. Being asked one day the secret of her sweet optimism, she replied, "I keep a pleasure book. Early in life, I resolved that every night I would record some pleasant experience which had come to me during the day. This has given me the habit of looking for the glad things instead of the sad ones in my life. And so, no matter how dark the clouds, I have always been able to see a bit of sunlight shining through."

Many days, she said, it was hard to see the light because she had had a large family, and had lost every member of it. In addition she had much illness, and many financial losses which left her very poor. But in spite of her afflictions and her poverty she had managed to find something to be thankful for every day of her life.

People who take life sadly, who see nothing "to rejoice and be glad" about, not only lose a tremendous amount of pleasure, real enjoyment, but they seriously cripple their ability and impair their success. They are not normal, and, therefore, cannot reach their maximum of strength and efficiency.

When I see people with gloomy minds attuned to sadness, who dwell exclusively on the serious side of life, I always feel like turning them around so that they will face towards the light, so that they will look at life in a hopeful, expectant, happy way, and let their shadows all fall behind them.

Mr. Schwab has always been a splendid example of the philosophy of happiness. He is one of the happiest men I have ever met! In his younger days when he was struggling to get a foothold in business he was always bubbling over with happiness. This constant flow of good spirits was one of the first things that attracted Mr. Carnegie's attention. In the days of strike troubles at the Homestead works it was young Schwab's merry temper that kept Mr. Carnegie from giving way to serious despondency. When the ironmaster felt very blue over the situation, the young man would sing Scotch songs for him and cheer him up, so that Mr. Carnegie would slap him on the shoulder and say, "You're all right, Charles, you're all right!"

Over-seriousness depresses the mental faculties and tends to lower efficiency. It is the man who sings at his work, the one who is bubbling over with gladness, with a sense of abounding vitality that is the normal, healthful, successful man.

Life should be full of play, even of fun, full of light and cheer. It would be if we knew how to live. If, like the old lady who kept the pleasure book, and Pollyanna, the glad girl, we make a habit of looking for something to be glad about, we shall very soon master the secret of happiness.

Let us "rejoice and be glad." Let us cry with Pollyanna, "Just be glad – that's the game."

4
DISCOURAGEMENT, A DISEASE HOW TO CURE IT.

DISCOURAGEMENT FLIES before the thought of God, when we become conscious of our partnership with Him.

Eight hundred and sixty men, women and children on the average in New York City commit suicide every year – much more than two a day. In one year Bellevue Hospital treated two hundred and thirty-five people who had tried to kill themselves. In other large cities of the world the suicide toll is even larger than in New York.

It is estimated that more than fifteen thousand people commit suicide each year in the United States. In the entire civilized world, a million people each year – more than five hundred a day – are guilty of self-destruction!

Just think of the tragedy of it, – one suicide every three minutes somewhere on the earth!

Since life is so precious to the normal man that even the basest criminals count the days and the hours before their execution, dreading the cutting off of life even in a prison cell, why do so many people take their own lives?

Because they are discouraged.

The psychological aspect of the suicide has never been properly studied, but in nine cases out of ten, if not in every case, discouragement is the cause of self-destruction.

Not long ago a young musician in New York, in a fit of despondency, committed suicide. He was so poor that he had been obliged to pawn his violin. Discouraged at his lack of success and filled with fear at the possibility of not being able to redeem his beloved violin, which was a very rare one, he decided that life under such conditions was not worth living, and then and there ended it.

These crises on the mental or physical plane are a part of every life. How we meet them is the test of our courage, the measure of our faith in God and our conscious oneness with Him.

In a description of his sensations under fire a British officer fighting in northern France in the great war said, "There's a good deal of rot talked of heroism at present. If it is all true, there are many millions of heroes in Europe just now, and I leave that to you. I've found it harder to go straight in life than to go under fire."

We are "under fire" all our lives, and the real hero is the one who keeps straight on in spite of discouragements and disappointments, never losing one jot of heart or courage, never giving way to despair, trusting always in the Divine Power that will lead him to his goal.

Many a talented young artist has given up in despair because critics discouraged him, told him, perhaps, that he did not belong to any established school, and that if he did not follow the conventional rules of art he would not be recognized. These discouraged souls did not realize that the one who listens to the voice in his own soul, and who, trusting to the power within, blazes a new path, is the one who most certainly attains distinction.

When Ole Bull first came to this country, musical critics said he would make no great impression here. They predicted that his American debut would be a failure because he violated so many of the laws of musical composition, that a certain violinist, popular at the time, was head and shoulders above him and that he would stand no chance in competition with him. The name of that man who was so technically perfect, but who lacked Ole Bull's soul, is not known to the public today, while the name of Ole Bull is enshrined immortally in the minds of American people – in the minds of all peoples.

Discouragement is one of the greatest of human enemies. It is an unmitigated curse. It has done more to dwarf the efforts of the race, has thwarted more careers, stunted and starved more lives, ruined more creative power than any other one agent. It is a disease that is well-nigh universal in some form. Everybody suffers more or less from it, is the victim of its poison. It bombards us from within and without.

There are always plenty of people who will attack you from without, who will see reasons why you will not succeed in your undertaking, who will tell you that it is impossible to overcome the obstacles in your way, and unless you have a sublime faith in yourself and a resolution which knows no retreat, which takes no backward steps, you are likely to become discouraged and then sidetracked.

Discouragement, however, comes most frequently from within, and causes more poverty and crime than almost any other one thing. It is an indirect producer of poverty, because it paralyzes ability and blights efficiency. A person is in no position to produce anything when his mind is full of doubt and fear. When suffering from discouragement one's whole being is negative, demoralized. Courage, the leader of the mental faculties, is paralyzed, and the judgment is not sound. No man is level headed when he is discouraged or blue. He is in no condition to look squarely at an issue, because his reasoning powers are dulled and his enthusiasm is dampened. In other words, there is anarchy in the whole mental kingdom and, until the order is restored and courage again leads the way, the faculties will not respond with their best.

This was recently illustrated by the suicide of a man who feared he could not raise the thirteen thousand dollars he believed he needed to save himself from ruin. In settling up his estate, however, it was found that the man was not in straitened circumstances and did not really need any such amount to keep his business going.

Time and again it has been found that people who lost heart under fire were just this side of victory over their difficulties when they threw down their weapons and gave up the battle in despair. How often has a letter or a telegram with good news that would have heartened and encouraged a discouraged one to fight on, come just after the sufferer had ended it all! How often has a friend bearing relief come just after the irrevocable deed had been done!

Yet we continue to read daily in the newspapers of people, young and old, who lose faith and commit suicide because of failure in business, loss of property, loss of friends, trouble in the home, disappointment in love – for a thousand and one reasons. But they may nearly all be summed up under the one head – discouragement.

And what is this Moloch to which so many lives are sacrificed? It is simply a diseased mind. Discouragement is a mental disease. It is just as truly a disease as smallpox, typhoid, scarlet fever, or any other ailment which physicians diagnose as physical disease. Discouragement is much worse than any of these because it so often unbalances the sufferer and drives him to crime, or to drink and consequent failure and misery.

A letter just received from a young man who is undergoing a term of imprisonment for robbery shows how easily discouragement drives some minds off the right path.

"When we make our slips, our bad breaks and unfortunate ventures, our bad decisions," he writes, "we are in a more or less discouraged, despondent and unbalanced state, and are willing to do almost anything to get rid of our fears and anxieties for the moment. When our minds are negative we are always cowards."

This young man had been out of work for a long time, and when a shiftless station agent with whom he was acquainted loaned him his keys, he stole a book of Wells Fargo Express money orders from the station and succeeded in passing some of them before he was arrested. He says that the awful price he has had to pay for his slip has taught him that it is infinitely easier to do right than wrong, and that when he leaves prison he is determined to do his best to redeem his past.

Another young man who was on the verge of discouragement tells how he was turned right about face by the appearance and the story of one who had fallen a victim to the discouragement disease.

This young man who was in business in New York had had such a severe setback when the Great War broke out that he was just ready to give up the struggle. Quite disheartened he sat down one day on a bench in Madison Square to decide just how he would wind up the business in which he had practically failed and also to decide what he would do next.

While sitting there thinking the matter over a ragged, dejected tramp came along and sat down beside him. The man was evidently a victim of drink and all sorts of dissipation, and looked as though he was near a complete collapse.

The young man, noticing his companion's wretched appearance, asked him how he happened to be in such a predicament. The tramp, whose quick intelligence saw at once that there was something very serious on his questioner's mind, instead of replying to his question asked him in turn what his trouble was.

The young man frankly confessed that his business was ruined, and that he didn't know what he was going to do. Then the tramp looking him straight in the eye said: "My friend, do you realize how rich you are compared with me?

"You have youth, health, and strength. Your vitality has not been sapped by dissipation. You have everything to live for, and as you value your life, don't give way to discouragement. That was what ruined me. I am a well-educated man, and was once a prosperous one. But years ago, after a business failure, in such a crisis as you are now facing, I lost my pluck and thought whiskey would brace me up, temporarily, until I could get on my feet again. It did. I had never drank before, and at first it seemed to me that I had found a very valuable aid, something which would give me courage, strength, initiative, something which would help me to dare to take chances, which I had previously shrunk from. For a time whiskey seemed to me to be the elixir of life.

"It braced up all my faculties and, apparently, doubled my brain power. But I had to keep increasing the quantity I took to get the desired effects, and then all at once I found my will power was weakening, and the courage which whiskey had temporarily stimulated gradually lessened until I had less than before. Then I began to see what whiskey was really doing and resolved many times to quit it. But the awful craving, the cruel thirst for drink, together with my increasing despondency and weakened will power, got the better of me and I drank again and again until I could not quit. And now, look at me! I am a wreck, without hope, without a future!

"But you have most of your life before you and really have nothing to be discouraged about. You have done nothing dishonest or disgraceful. The only disgrace is in quitting after failure. And there is no failure that cannot be retrieved. Men who have done great things, made stepping stones of their failures. The disgrace is not in falling, but in not rising every time you fall.

Brace up, and remember that, 'Not failure, but low aim is crime."

The young man was deeply impressed by the story of his unfortunate companion. The evidences of superior intelligence and education still manifest in the poor human wreck appalled him, and he said to himself, "If this unhappy wretch can still look at life in that way, can see its great possibilities, there is certainly something left for me." And after doing what he could to help the man who had tried to help him, he went out of Madison Square a new man, with new resolution in his face, a new courage and determination in his heart.

He is now a prosperous man, and he says, "I attribute a large part of my success to the stimulus imparted at a critical moment by that unfortunate fellow who had given way to discouragement and sacrificed everything that life held dear to the thing which had enslaved him."

Victims of discouragement little realize the tremendous damage they are doing to themselves when they allow this fatal enemy of their happiness, and their efficiency, to get lodgment in their mind. Nobody does good work when discouraged. There is no spontaneity in it, no resourcefulness, no inventiveness, no originality, and no enthusiasm. It is mechanical, life-less.

The moment you yield to discouragement all your mental faculties become depressed. You lose power. Your initiative is paralyzed, your executive ability strangled. You are in no condition to do anything effectively. Your whole mentality is placed at a tremendous disadvantage, and until this enemy is driven out of your mind, neutralized by the affirmation and the contemplation of its opposites – of courage, cheer, hope, and a vigorous expectation of splendid things to come – you are in no condition to do good work.

Every suggestion of discouragement, of fear of failure, is a destructive force, and in the degree that we allow ourselves to be influenced by it will it tear down and retard our life processes, our life work. It will darken the mind and cause one to make fatally wrong decisions, to take steps which may ruin one's happiness, one's whole life.

Many divorces are the result of unfortunate decisions to marry when girls were discouraged, when they could not see any other way out of their difficulties. I have known of many girls, after some great sorrow had come to them, marrying men whom they could never have been induced to marry in happier days. They had lost a mother, or a father, or some calamity had overtaken the family, and the girls consented to marry men they did not love in order to relieve the suffering of those dear to them, or because there seemed to be no other resource for themselves in a difficult situation. They were willing to do anything to get rid of the thing that was perplexing and troubling them at the time. Like sufferers from sea sickness they felt their troubles never would pass away.

It is characteristic of seasickness that the victim cannot see any end to his misery. Try as he will to imagine himself well in so many days or hours, he cannot do it. This hopelessness is in some degree characteristic of sick people generally. They cannot seem to picture themselves as strong and well again. When suffering extreme pain of any sort, such as a severe toothache, for instance, it is difficult to believe that it will ever cease.

Still more difficult is it to try to picture an end to mental suffering. When trials and troubles come to us, when overwhelmed with sorrow, when death comes into our home and snatches away some dear one, it is very difficult to see through the storm, to pierce the black clouds and see the healing sun behind them. Struggling with the sorrow of that great loss in our life, it doesn't seem as though we could ever be happy again. When so suffering we wonder in a sort of dumb resentment how other people can possibly be laughing, having a good time, going to theaters, dances, enjoying life as usual. It seems cruel, almost, for others to enjoy when we feel as though we could never even smile again.

But we know that time heals the deepest sorrows, that physical and mental ills pass away, and that the brave soul is the one that adapts itself to the storms and sunshine of life.

Just as on a tropical summer day when the sun is suddenly blotted out of the heavens and the whole sky is so blackened by a sudden storm that we are obliged to light our homes and offices, and presently the clouds pass as quickly as they came and the sun blazes forth in all its glory just as though nothing had happened, so there come times in our lives when everything appears black and threatening, and then, suddenly, just as in nature, all becomes serene again.

The great thing for us to keep in mind when a life storm breaks is that, no matter how violent, it is only temporary and that behind the clouds the sun is always shining.

The new philosophy helps us to conquer discouragement by putting the emphasis on the right things, the things that are worthwhile. This is why we generally do not go to pieces when we happen to fail in our vocation. We have learned that material things are not the first essentials. We know that the great emphasis should be placed upon the life, the reality of man, which is divine. We know that a person can be a tremendous success although he has not a dollar in the world, though he has no home, no abiding place, no money, and dies in the poorhouse. In other words, the new philosophy teaches that real success does not consist in accumulating mere things.

It is a matter of personality and character. The accumulation of money is a side issue; the making of a living is a mere incidental to making a life. Time and again I have known people to go through what in the old thought would have been the most humiliating failures, failures which would probably have wrecked their lives and entirely destroyed their confidence in themselves. But in the new philosophy these things do not touch the soul. They are not realities in the highest sense.

None of Mr. Rockefeller's money touches the real Rockefeller. The reality of him is spiritual, is mental. It is mind, it is soul, it is God, and it is this reality of us that the new philosophy emphasizes.

God never intended that his children should go to pieces mentally and physically, be miserable and unhappy, that they should suffer mortification and chagrin when they have been honest and have done the best they could do, just because they have failed in their particular undertakings.

We were made to hold up our heads, to look the world in the face without flinching, as princes of the Most High. No matter what happens to our material possessions, if we have made good as men, as women, if we have been dead-in-earnest in delivering to the world the message we were sent here to deliver, there is no reason why we should feel humiliated or discouraged about anything.

There is only one thing that should make a man hang his head and feel humiliated, discouraged, only one thing that should make him wince when the world looks him in the face and that is his own wrong doing, his own sin.

There is a vast amount of splendid unused success material in the "down and outs," in the people who have lost their grip upon themselves because they have lost their courage. Some of them while out of work, suffering from discouragement, did something which caused them to lose their self-respect and now discouragement has become a disease with them. It has become chronic and no one can succeed with a discouraged mental attitude.

Courage is the leader in the mental realm, and when that is down all the other faculties drop in sympathy. Until courage says the word, neither initiative nor any of the other faculties will take a step forward. They refuse to work under discouragement. But when courage leads the way, all the others brace up and come to the rescue in team work.

What most people in the great failure army need is to have their courage restored, renewed. The discouraged have their backs turned toward the light, so that all the black shadows fall across their path. They are walking in their own shadows instead of in the glorious sun of God's light and love. Their disease has made them morbid. They need mental treatment, treatment that will let the light into their souls and show them what they still can do.

Emerson says, "What I need is somebody who will make me do what I can." What these discouraged ones need is somebody who can make them do what they can. They need to be turned around mentally. They need to be shown that they are not failures, but that they are mentally ill, sufferers from chronic discouragement.

There is one who can do this for you who are discouraged better than anyone else – your own higher self.

No matter how old you may be, or how depressing your present condition, if you take this other, higher self for your guide, you can recover your footing. And when you once get a glimpse of your real self, your real possibilities and assets, when you once get a glimpse of your divinity, and realize that you are a god in the making, that you are intended to be a glorious success instead of a miserable failure, you will jump back a quarter of a century or more and start life anew. Your courage will be restored and you will see life in a new light. You will see yourself as you never saw yourself before, you will get hold of yourself and your mental and physical resources as you never did before, you will make tremendous leaps forward. You will have a new motive for redeeming your past, you will have a new outlook on life, new hope; in other words, you will be a new creature. You will put off the old man, and never again will be content to grovel, never again be content with your second best. Then, only your highest and best will satisfy you, and you will strive to make your highest moments permanent. The very consciousness of having lost so many years will be an additional prod to your endeavor.

You can begin now to make good. Lift up your head and face toward the light. Quit fretting and complaining of your ill luck and be the poised, harmonious soul, the brave, successful, happy being the Creator planned. Cure yourself of your disease by conquering your mental enemies. You can drive out fear, worry, the "blues" and all discouragement, all the enemies of your success and happiness, by claiming your inheritance and asserting your kinship with God. Say to yourself:

"The truth of my being, the reality of me, is God. Why then should I be discouraged about anything? The Creator never intended me to express pessimism, doubt, discouragement or despondency, and I will have nothing more to do with them. I was intended to express joy and success, not gloom and failure. I am victory organized. I was planned to win out in life, not to be defeated. I was born for happiness, not for misery, for peace and serenity, not for perpetual anxiety and discouragement. There is something inside of me which tells me that I am bigger than circumstances, that nothing but my own consent can keep me in poverty and wretchedness, that there is no destiny which can keep me down, for I am my own destiny.

"I am a son of God, and I was never made to cower, to slink, to be discouraged, afraid of anything. I am one with my Father, and co-heir with Christ of all that He has. I do not fear want or failure. Fear is not an attribute of divinity, and has no place in my life. I am brave, courageous, a conqueror, and not a slave of circumstances. I am free and not bond. I will not allow my efficiency to be strangled, my hopes for the future blighted, my life to be spoiled by any form of discouragement or cowardice. I am courage, strength, confidence, masterfulness. Discouragement has no power over me, because it is not a reality. It is a mere bogey of the mind, a ghost of the imagination. This discouraged, yellow streak in my nature is really a reflection upon my Creator, an indication that I lack confidence in Him, that I am not sure that He can protect me. It is an intimation that I believe there is a greater power than His and that an evil one.

"No matter how many troubles or difficulties threaten, it is my business to trust, and not to fear, and from now on I shall do so. I shall hold a poised, serene mind, and shall lie down at night with confidence and assurance that my life, my welfare and my destiny are all in the hands of Him who controls everything and who doeth all things well."

Remember that whatever you dread, fear, you are attracting, because the mind always relates with whatever dominates the thought. That which we think most about we tend to get, and it is the easiest thing in the world to kill the possibility of realizing our ambitions and drawing to us the thing we fear by holding it in mind, by allowing doubt thoughts, anxious, discouraged thoughts to get possession of us and strangle our efficiency.

When in danger of giving way to discouragement, you will find a wonderful help in eliminating everything which stands between you and your Maker, and to allow free access to the flow of divine power. When one is thoroughly alive to the consciousness that he is supported by this divine power, in so far as he trusts it, and that it will rush to his assistance in any emergency or trouble, he is neither afraid nor discouraged.

All our discouragement and anxieties come from a feeling of separateness from our Creator and the consequent consciousness of weakness, of not being sufficiently protected, the feeling that we are standing alone. One who lives in conscious union with his Maker rises above disappointments and discouragements, and develops a hopeful, optimistic philosophy. Such a one sees in all his experiences, no matter how trying, growth and enlargement. He sees in the overcoming of life's problems an opportunity to become a full, complete man. He rises above circumstances, while those who do not see any saving, stimulating influences in their trials and disappointments are simply crushed by them.

What a superb sight is a soul who has ridden triumphantly through the storms of life, who has developed a beautiful, cheerful philosophy, who instead of being crushed by his trials and hardships has built them into a tower of hope and strength!

Compare such a man, who bears his burdens uncomplainingly, who laughs at difficulties and keeps pushing ahead as best he can, trying to make each day a real victory in his life, performing as nearly as possible a human being's ideal duty, to the one who curses his fate, rails at his ill luck, and grumbles at the burdens which are crushing him!

When things have gone wrong with you; when you are ready to give way to discouragement, think of these two pictures, and turn about face and vigorously assert your manhood or your womanhood. Declare your power to conquer your difficulty, whatever it may be. Say to yourself:

"Now it is right up to me to make good. I can't give way to discouragement, show the white feather, and yet keep my self-respect. I am able to overcome this thing; it has no power to keep me down. No matter whether I can see the way out or not I shall trust in God, keep going, and forge ahead. No matter what opposes, I shall keep the rudder of my ship headed toward the port.

"I will quit this everlasting self-depreciation, for it is a crime against my Maker as well as myself, and I will believe that what the Creator has made and pronounced good is so. I am done with this putting myself on a bargain counter. I am no longer going about the earth making the impression that I have a skim-milk opinion of myself. No more of the poorhouse attitude for me. There are better things waiting for me than that. I am a prince, and I have inherited princely things. I have a princely inheritance.

"I know that every time I say 'I can't do this,' or 'I can't do that,' 'I can't afford this,' or 'I can't afford that,' I undermine my power. Hereafter I am going to deal in positives, in affirmations of power – 'I can,' 'I will,' 'I am able.' Henceforth I will have nothing to do with negatives that tear down, destroy.

"If I am part of Reality; if I have existed millions of years, and will continue to exist for untold ages to come; if my existence is from everlasting to everlasting, why should I be anxious, alarmed? Why should I be perturbed about temporary happenings, the mere accidents of everyday life? They have no power over me. I am a part of the divine Entity. My being is beyond the possibility of destruction or change. There is something in me that is absolutely indestructible, and I shall not get into a flurry of uneasiness, become discouraged by what I can really control. I know I am anchored eternally. Therefore, I will allow nothing to trouble or disturb me. Henceforth nothing will. I stand firm in this resolve."

Multitudes of people find great help and comfort in repeating such Bible promises as these: "He that dwelleth in the secret place of the Most High shall abide under the shadow of the Almighty." "He shall cover thee with his feathers, and under his wings shalt thou trust; his truth shall be thy shield and buckler." "There shall no evil befall thee, neither shall any plague come nigh thy dwelling."

What a solvent for discouragement and the "blues," what a healing for all heart hurts are found in these wonderful promises!

The habit of driving out of our consciousness every suggestion of failure, of disappointment, of discouragement or evil by substituting its opposite is of inestimable value. The ability to do this, to clarify the mind of everything which can possibly injure it, is the secret of all success and happiness.

The scientific fact that the mind cannot contain at the same moment opposite thoughts or emotions makes us absolute masters of our fate. To live upward or downward, to be a success or a failure is simply a matter of choice. It all depends on the suggestions we assimilate, the kind of thought we prefer.

We can allow ourselves to be overwhelmed by discouragement, or we can rise above it, just as we decide. It is natural for all of us to think of the wonderful things we would do if we could only get rid of the things that block our way and defeat our possible successes. If we did not have to struggle with disappointments, with heartaches, with trials and troubles of all sorts, what a triumphant journey life would be! Yet the real test of your bigness is whether or not you will fulfill your ambition to the letter, whether you will carry out your great life plan grandly and superbly regardless of things that are apparently trying to down you.

Nothing will help more to overcome discouragement than the suggestion of courage or success. The constructive force of the positive thought will not only drive out the negative thought, but it will up build and strengthen all the faculties.

Every human being can increase his courage and multiply his strength by frequently saying to himself: "I am a child of the King of Kings, and have nothing to fear. If I always do the best I can in all circumstances, there is no reason why I should ever be anxious about the results. I shall not. I am courage, I am success. Nothing can harm me because I am one with the One, I cannot want, I cannot fail, because I am in touch with the Infinite Source of all life."

5
THE FORCE THAT MOVES MOUNTAINS

FAITH MOVES mountains.

"To him that believeth, all things are possible." The man who does not believe in something and believe in it with all his soul is a pretty poor stick.

Let nothing undermine your faith in your ultimate triumph. Hold this tenaciously, vigorously, intensely, and after awhile you will see things coming your way. Don't be afraid to think too highly of yourself. If the Creator made you and is not ashamed of the job, certainly you should not be. He pronounced His work good, and you should respect it.

Faith increases confidence, carries conviction, multiplies ability. Faith doesn't think or guess. It sees the way out. It is not discouraged or blinded by mountains of difficulties, because it sees through them – sees the goal beyond.

There are marvelous utilities, infinite good and unspeakable beauties in the great cosmic intelligence, the unseen world, ready for our use and enjoyment. If we only had sufficient faith to believe they were there we could draw them to ourselves.

Writing of heroes discovered by the world war, Edmund Riemper Broadus says:

"There are stories of the heroism of 'our boys' that stir us beyond words – stories, too, that change with astonishing abruptness our estimates of those whom we had too lightly regarded. There was a certain youth, for example, for whom I fear that I had scant respect during his student life; a sickly fellow with rather a hang-dog air. He was out of his classes a good deal of the time and he was not successful in examinations. I believe that I suspected him of malingering. He tried to enlist and was turned down by the medical inspector, and tried again and yet again without success.

How he ever got in, nobody could understand; but one day he went, and we shook our heads and prophesied that he would be incapacitated in a week or two. We heard no more of him until word came in letters from his friends that he had quietly picked up a smoking bomb and thrown it clear of the trench before it exploded, and then had climbed out in the face of the flying bullets and brought in a wounded comrade. And this was he who had only last year seemed such a faint-hearted traveler along life's common way!"

Every now and then, like this writer, we are amazed at some youth we knew, starting out all at once and doing some tremendous thing which we did not believe was possible to him. He may not have had any more ability, perhaps not as much, as those around him, but he had a superb self-faith, which enabled him to dare and do, when the more timid ones, even perhaps, with far superior ability, hesitated, wavered, did not dare to attempt what in reality they were able to do.

It is faith that everywhere does the "impossible." It is faith in God and faith in oneself, a divine self-confidence that makes men gods, whose will must be obeyed.

If it were not for wrong thinking such faith would be the rule in human life instead of the exception, for "God hath not given us the spirit of fear; but of power, and of love, and of a sound mind." Unfortunately most of us measure ourselves by our weakness instead of by our strength. We estimate ourselves at our worst instead of our best. We seem to think that the vision of ourselves we see in our optimistic, hopeful, uplifted moments is a mere mirage of the imagination, and not our real selves.

Comparatively few people realize how much self-faith has to do with achievement. The great majority never seem to think that it is a real creative force. Yet faith is not only a real power, but one of the greatest we know. In fact, men do great things in proportion to the intensity and the persistency of their faith.

When Goliath, the great giant of Gath, came to the Israelite camp, with his pretentious boasting, challenging the Israelites to select a man to fight with him, to determine whether they or the Philistines should be conquerors, the Israelites were so terrified that none dared offer to do battle with him.

Later, when he returned to repeat his challenge, a mere youth, David, heard his boasting, and took up his challenge. After much pleading with his elders for the privilege, the youth was allowed to go fight the giant. They insisted, however, on putting him in heavy armor, as a protection for his body, and placing a sword in his hand before he went to meet his foe. But he said to them: "I am not used to these things, I cannot fight with these handicaps. These are not my weapons. I have other weapons with which to fight the giant." So he took off all of his armor and went forth with no other weapon than a simple sling and a few pebbles which he took from the brook.

When the giant leader of the Philistines, protected from head to foot with armor, armed with mighty weapons, and preceded by his shield bearer, saw the unarmed and unprotected Israelite youth approaching, he was angry at being so insulted, and said to him, "Come to me and I will give thy flesh unto the fowls of the air, and to the beasts of the field."

The undaunted youth answered: "Thou comest to me with a sword and with a spear, and with a shield; but I come to thee in the name of the Lord of hosts, the God of the armies of Israel whom thou hast defied. This day will the Lord deliver thee into mine hand."

David did not, like the Philistine, put his faith in armor, in sword, or in shield, but in the Almighty; and by faith he conquered his mighty foe. Putting a single stone in his sling he buried it in the forehead of the giant, who fell prostrate to the ground.

Faith is the very pith and marrow of achievement.

No faith, no achievement.

All-absorbing faith, great achievement.

Show me a great achiever and I will show you a man of great faith, faith in himself, in his ability to achieve his aim. Faith has ever been the miracle worker of the ages. It is the connecting link between God and man; it is man's strength, the cornerstone of all his building, all his achieving.

The trouble with those of us who are not doing what we can and ought to do is that we lack faith. We do not believe that we can go into the great within of us and simply and naturally make connection with divine force, with the all-supply, with the Power that made us, that Power which has created and which upholds the universe and from which we derive our strength.

We make this connection through faith. This is our trolley pole, and if we could only put it up until it taps the wire which carries omnipotent power we should feel the thrill of divine life, of inexhaustible strength surging through us.

If you do not make this connection; if you lack the divine self-confidence born of faith in Omnipotence, you will never be what you long to be. Your prayers will come back to you unanswered; your efforts will bear no fruit; your negative attitude will make it impossible for you to achieve your object.

A negative, doubting mind, a mind saturated with fear of failure can no more accomplish, create, or produce, anything of value than a stone can violate the law of gravitation by flying up in the air. The Creator does not change the law of gravitation because a man walks off the roof of a house, even though he may do it unconsciously, in his sleep. The creative principle, the law of achievement, does not vary any more than the law of gravitation, and you will achieve what you desire, be what you long to be, only when you obey the law. The Creator himself cannot fulfill your desire in any other way, any more than He can make the sun, contrary to law, turn from its course in the heavens, any more than He could make the world turn about and go in the opposite direction around the sun, when the heavenly bodies are pulling it the other way.

There is all the difference in the world between the power of the person who believes in his destiny, who has unquestioned faith in his mission, who believes that he is a part of the divine plan, that he is in the current which runs Godward, and the one who does not have this faith. The one is equipped for a victorious life; the other is headed toward defeat.

It is always the men and the women with a stupendous faith, a colossal self-confidence, that do the great deeds, accomplish the "impossible." Those who do not take much stock in themselves, who have only a sort of milk-and-water purpose, who do not believe that they were intended to do anything in particular, never have been and never will be the doers of the world.

I have before me a letter from a young woman, who says she never expects to amount to anything or to accomplish much of anything. "I have always been unlucky, a blunderer," she writes. "I am always making mistakes, and nearly always fail in whatever I undertake to do. I never have had any confidence in myself, and I fear I never will."

Now, the reason why this girl fails to accomplish anything is very clear. Her mental attitude is the main cause of her trouble. No one can succeed with such a mental attitude as hers, for achievement is first mental. It begins in the mind.

There is no philosophy, no power in the universe that can help me to do a thing when I think I can't do it.

More people make wrecks of their lives from lack of faith in themselves than from any other cause. There is only now and then a man who really believes in his own bigness, who has sufficient faith to back up his ability. And ability must be backed up by a superb self-confidence before it can accomplish anything. The ability of a Napoleon or a Webster would be absolutely powerless without self-confidence.

Before we can win out in life we must believe in our power to win. We must be confident in our expectations of success, vigorous in our self faith. We must believe in ourselves and the thing we are doing without reserve, with all our hearts.

When Jane Addams left college she was in such poor health that physicians told her she could not live more than six months. "All right," she said, "I will take that six months to get as near as I can to the one thing I want to do for humanity."

Can anyone doubt that Miss Addams' restoration to health and the great work she has accomplished for humanity in founding and conducting Hull House, with its many beneficent activities, in the long years since the physicians gave her only six months more of life, are due to her deep faith in God and the divine power within herself?

The Centurion said to Christ: "Speak the word only and my servant shall be healed." And when he returned home he found his servant healed. When he asked at what hour he had begun to improve they told him it was at the seventh hour – the very hour at which he had talked with the Christ. The Centurion's was the faith that makes miracles possible.

Lack of faith is the supreme cause of failure. How can anyone accomplish anything worthwhile when one's very executive power is paralyzed, disheartened, discouraged by the thought, amounting almost to a certainty, of failure? It would be to overcome or to set aside the working of the law of cause and effect. Your achievement will never rise above your faith. That is the high-water mark of your attainment.

I have seen a man of ordinary strength who was hypnotized, stretched between two chairs, with his heels resting on one chair and his head on another, holding up six or eight men on that part of his body which lay between the chairs. This man supported a horse in the same way. Now, where did this extraordinary increase of power come from? It only lasted while the hypnotist made his subject believe that he could support the men and the horse. The moment the hypnotist shook the man's confidence in himself, shattered his faith that he could bear up the enormous weight laid on him, the man dropped to the floor. And when the hypnotist made him believe that he could not bear up a single man, he could not do it. In fact, under this influence of hypnotic suggestion he could not even support his own body.

We never can get farther than our faith in ourselves. We cannot do anything bigger than we think we can. We are hemmed in by our opinion of ourselves, and until we enter that larger atmosphere of faith where we shall find the belief that we can do the thing we were made to do beating within us, we cannot do it.

A hypnotist could make a Webster, or a Shakespeare, believe he was a fool. He could make a Sandow believe that he could not lift a chair, and the man, strong as he is, couldn't do so simple a thing as this until his faith and self-confidence were restored.

Now the power which enables a man to obey the command or suggestion of a hypnotist to do things easily which in his conscious state would be impossible does not come from the hypnotist. It was in the subject himself all the time. The hypnotist merely aroused him, made the man believe he could do the thing suggested, and he did it.

Muscles that are trained to lift and support enormous weights receive the most of their power from the mind of the athlete. The same muscles, if separated from the mind that controls them, if taken from the man's body, could not support a tenth part of the weight without breaking.

Experiments have shown that the deltoid muscle, taken immediately from an athlete's arm at the moment of an accidental death, would sustain only about fifty pounds of weight before it would break, while just before the man's death this same muscle would have supported hundreds of pounds. This great difference had a mental cause. It was the athlete's self-confidence that added all the extra power. As a matter of fact a man could not hold up his hand if he did not believe he could do so, if he had not confidence that he had the strength to do it.

The size of our faith indicates the size of the cable which connects us with our Maker. If this faith cable, which carries the omnipotent current, is small we get but a little of the force from the mighty current that runs heavenward.

If our faith were large enough we should be larger men and women, and we should travel Godward infinitely faster than we do.

One reason why many people do not amount to more than they do is that they seem to look upon their life dream, their ambition as a sort of fanciful mental picture, something that has no definite basis in reality. These people never take their life mission very seriously, and consequently never grow to their full stature. They do not seem to grasp the unity of God's plan, or to realize that they were meant to play definite and distinct individual parts in it. Yet that is just what we are here to do. We were not thrown off as independent, unrelated units of the universe.

There is still just as vital a connection between ourselves and our Maker as there is between the branch and the vine. We are a projection of His mind, a definite part of His plan, and our ambitions, our longings, are in a way a reflection of the universal plan. Those who have faith in themselves feel that their ambitions are evidences of ability to back them by accomplishment, to make their dreams realities.

Abraham Lincoln was a very modest, unassuming man, but when the first rumblings of the Civil War reverberated through the North and a presidential election was near at hand, the Spirit moved him to put himself forward as leader of the nation. When the politicians were looking round for a suitable man for that great position, Lincoln asked them why they did not nominate him. He said he felt within his breast the power to carry the nation through the threatened crisis, and that he believed he would be elected. Coming from a less modest man this assurance would look like a boast, but Lincoln's motives were pure, and his faith, based upon a marvelous fitness for the work to be done, carried him to success.

The history makers have ever had overmastering convictions in regard to their life work. They have believed in their vision and the part they were to play. They have believed that their ambition foreshadowed a prophecy; that it was the substance of things expected, and not a mere figment of the imagination. In other words, men who have won out in the world have been profound believers in their destiny.

The faith of such men impresses us with a conviction of their power. We all feel that there is something about the man who believes in his destiny that commands our respect, our homage. The world itself makes way for the man who believes he was born to play a grand part in the human drama. The world makes way for such a man or such a woman as it made way for the peasant maid of Orleans.

Practically all of Joan of Arc's miraculous power over the French army was due to her conviction of a divine call to free her country from its enemies. But for this conviction she would have carried no more weight than an ordinary soldier. Indeed, but for her faith in the divine call she never would have reached Charles the Dauphin, never obtained his consent to take the chief command of his army. She got her commission from him "by taking the positive stand that she was the one person who could save France – that she had the consummate courage of a whole army in herself – that she knew beyond doubt that the army under her leadership would be victorious."

From the time when, a little girl tending her father's sheep, she first heard the call in her soul her faith was unshakable. What good did it do for Joan's father to threaten to drown his daughter if she persisted in her silly dreams that she was to liberate France? What effect had ridicule, especially the coarse ridicule of her sex by the soldiers, on her deep-rooted conviction? Was there ever anything more foolish than that a simple peasant maid who tended sheep on a farm, and who had never been away from home, or had the slightest military training or knowledge of war tactics, could lead a defeated army to victory? How did she treat all such questioning, ridicule, abuse and contempt? Her supreme faith ameliorated them all. They left her absolutely unmoved.

By faith alone the simple maid performed one of the greatest miracles of history. No human being even with the mental power of a Napoleon, without a superb military training, could have performed the miracle which this uneducated, untrained peasant girl performed.

What good did it do for the wise men of Italy and Spain to laugh at Columbus, and to picture at their meeting in court, men standing on their heads, and everything, including his ships, falling off the edge of the earth if it were round, and revolved, as Columbus claimed? The more these men laughed at him, the stronger grew his faith in his mission, and the more determined he became to prove the truth of his claim. And the mutinous crew of Columbus, after many weary weeks' wandering on an apparently limitless ocean, met with the same immovable faith, the same stubborn resolution, when they threatened to put their leader in chains. Day after day on this memorable voyage we find this entry in his log book, "This day we sailed west because it was our course."

What hardship, what persecution, what ridicule, or contempt, what denunciation even of those who knew him best could have induced such a man to give up his voyage of discovery? Although no geographer had ever referred to any land on the other side of the globe, and no scientist had hinted at such a thing, nothing could turn Columbus from his purpose because there was that something in him which looked beyond insuperable obstacles, beyond every objection, and saw land beyond the seas. It was this faith born in the divine within of him, this faith back of the flesh but not of it, which sustained him in all his trials, both before and after his great discovery.

The men who have left their mark on the world have had a faith which nothing could shake. Not the direst poverty, the most inhospitable treatment, not cruelty, not ridicule could separate them from their belief in their mission and their resolve to carry it out.

When a man's faith in himself and in his mission is the dominant note in his life, nothing can daunt him, no power can keep him from his own. Think of the faith which Peary exhibited before he discovered the North Pole! Time and time again he tried to find it, risking life and all his resources in the search. The loss of his ship, the loss of his men, and his own scores of hair-breadth escapes did not daunt him, could not shake his faith. The North Pole was written in Peary's heart. He must discover it. Nothing could turn him from his object. Many a time his friends pleaded with the explorer not to risk his life again, but to no purpose. "To the North Pole" was the slogan which haunted him day and night until at last he found it.

Faith is the force that moves mountains, that has ever performed the miracles of civilization. What incredible things, "impossible" things, have been done in the world's history by souls aroused to a sense of their own power! Who can ever estimate what the mental attitude of self-confidence has accomplished! Who can figure what the world has lost from the inaction or the failure of people with splendid ability, men and women who had no faith in themselves, who were so filled with doubt of their own power that their initiative was discouraged and their creative ability killed!

There are thousands of people in very ordinary positions today, who are not only capable of filling much higher ones, but who would actually be advanced if they only had sufficient faith in themselves to branch out and compete for the superior place. There are men in all sorts of inferior positions who, in many instances, are abler than the managers and superintendents over them, but who do not know their strength, because they have never tested it.

Not long ago a friend of mine, a comparatively young man, was unexpectedly called to fill temporarily a position much above his own, which had suddenly become vacant. So well, however, did he fulfill the duties of the higher place that he was complimented by his employers and retained in the position.

This man had been working for a small salary for years, and said that he had never dreamed of being advanced so suddenly. In fact, he had begun to have a feeling that he did not amount to much, that he was a kind of failure anyway. He knew he had ability in certain directions, hut he did not dare to start or to go ahead with anything. All these years his lack of confidence in himself had acted upon his great ability like an anchor to a balloon. But when he found that he was really capable of assuming a great responsibility; when level-headed business men showed their belief in him by entrusting him with the handling of a large business, his power was trebled. His awakened faith in himself made a man of him. He began to think he amounted to something; that he was somebody after all, and thereafter he advanced by leaps and bounds.

It makes a tremendous difference how you approach your life work, whether you come to it with a superb faith in yourself, an unshakable belief in the Power that sustains you, and a firm determination to make a triumphant success of it, or whether you come to it with a faint heart, a doubting, wavering mind, and weak endeavor.

The timid, fearful, questioning, "What if I should fail?" attitude has ruined more careers than anything else. On the other hand, there is everything in holding the courageous, self-confident thought. We fail only when we have lost our grip on ourselves, lost our faith in our ability to succeed. We could all do infinitely more than we have done, or are doing, if we only had enough faith in ourselves to undertake what we long to do. New strength comes to the man or woman who dares to begin.

It is through faith we touch the very source of life. It is the key which unlocks the door to power. Faith opens the door to the great within, where principle dwells, where strength is generated. If we could measure a man's faith we could come very near to predicating accurately the measure of his success in life.

It is not what other people say of you, but something you feel, inside of you, that you are capable of doing. This is your pattern, your model. Your true model is the one you see when you are the most optimistic, and not the mean diminutive figure of yourself which you see when you have on your pessimistic spectacles.

"Nothing in life is more remarkable than the unnecessary anxiety which we endure and generally occasion ourselves," said Benjamin Disraeli, a man who had attained the lofty position of Prime Minister of England, in spite of difficulties that would have completely vanquished a timid, unbelieving, worrying soul. It was his unconquerable faith in himself that raised the once despised Jew to the proudest place in England – next to Queen Victoria, who honored him as a personal friend.

Disraeli, who was made Earl of Beaconsfield by his queen, is a splendid example of the tremendous force of the miracle-producing power of self faith, of the conviction that one is born to do great things or to become a man of power and influence. Even in the face of disappointment, failure, and ridicule, the young Jew never lost faith in himself, never swerved in his purpose to be the great political leader of England.

Whatever other weaknesses, defects or deficiencies successful men have had they have all had a powerful conviction of their ability to perform the things they have undertaken.

One of the chief factors in Colonel Roosevelt's many-sided success has been his superb faith in Theodore Roosevelt. Nothing has ever undermined that faith. No abuse, no lying about him, no criticism has ever shaken his belief in himself. Nothing that has ever come his way has phased him, because he has felt equal to any task thrust upon him.

Now, suppose Roosevelt had this one lack in his nature, the lack of confidence, of faith in himself, with the same ability, the same opportunities, the same favoring environment he has had – what would have been the result? He probably never would have been heard from outside of his own country. His career has been built on self-faith. He early learned to believe in Roosevelt. He knew that he had ability, and that by training and making the most of it he could do what other people could do, what others had done, under similar or far less favorable conditions. It is this superb self-faith which has always characterized him, that has made him so striking a figure in our national life. Had Mr. Roosevelt lacked this one element, the effectiveness of his natural ability, if not completely nullified, would in every respect have been cut down tremendously.

Our flag says to the American people, "I am what you have made me. I am just as great and no greater than you believe me to be. I stand for what you think I stand for. I cannot rise above your estimate of me. What you think of me I am. I typify your thought of me. If you put a high value upon human liberty, upon democracy, upon human rights, then that is what I mean, that is what I typify. I am that which you think I am."

The same thing is true of ourselves. What we impress upon our subconscious self, our estimate of our ability, our talent, our initiative, is what we will express in life; is what we will represent not only to ourselves, but to others. The sort of picture other people carry of you in their mind is pretty nearly the sort of man you believe yourself to be. And the sort of picture others hold of you will react upon you to strengthen your own mental picture, your own estimate of yourself, whatever it may be.

The world classifies men by their faith in themselves, in their mission in life, their faith in what they undertake to do. The man who lacks faith in himself inspires no faith in others.

The psychology of faith is one of the most interesting studies in human nature. Faith is the spiritual faculty which runs ahead, the courier which shows the way, the general which encourages the men in the army; it is the commander who gets wireless messages from a higher source. Faith is the Napoleon in the mental kingdom. All the other faculties are like the soldiers in Napoleon's army, – their power is multiplied many times by their faith in their leader. They will follow faith to the death, but when faith wavers, when doubt takes the helm, it is all up. There is no more fight. That means retreat. He can who thinks he can, and he can't who thinks he can't. No one can advance farther than his faith in himself and in his mission. Self-faith leads in every great achievement.

Even when others cry "Impossible," the man supported by faith persists, and achieves his object.

Faith puts us in touch with infinite power, opens the way to unbounded possibilities, limitless achievement. Faith does not think or guess; it knows, for it sees the way out. It is the one thing that we can be sure will not mislead us. Our faith is not a mere empty fancy; it is a positive substance, a real creative force, a force which produces. St. Paul saw this great force back of a powerful faith, when he said, "Faith is the substance of things hoped for."

Consider the marvelous power of St. Paul's faith! It gripped every fiber of his being. Every drop of blood in him seemed to tug away at his one unwavering aim – to convert the world to Christianity. A similar thing is true of Martin Luther. What power or influence could have shaken Luther from his mighty purpose? When he nailed his theses on the church door it was war to the death if necessary.

Nothing has ever been so bitterly assailed, so stubbornly fought against, so abused as the Christian religion. No book was ever published that the world has tried so hard to blot out as the Bible, and yet no other book has anything like such a sale as the Bible. Even today the sales of "best sellers" look small in comparison with the sale of this book which the world has tried to destroy. And it is faith only that has enabled this Christian philosophy to survive the frightful attacks made upon it.

It was by faith that the Christian religion was established and that Christ's teachings survived the determination of the great Roman Empire, then at the zenith of its power, to crush them. Just picture the enormous disproportion between that little band of Christ and His followers and the great Roman Empire, which was determined to destroy them! Yet that mighty empire crumbled, while Christ's teachings endure and the religion He established spreads to every remotest corner of the earth!

Think of the first little company of the early Christians, unarmed, unaided, pitted against the power of ancient Rome. Persecuted, thrown into the arena in the Coliseum, to be torn to pieces by wild animals; dipped in tar and used as torches to light up the lake in front of Nero's palace, they suffered without a murmur! What enabled these men and women to persist against such enormous odds? A mighty faith which no power on earth could shake.

Think you the early Christian martyrs could have gone serenely to the stake, and could have declared their faith without a sign of wavering, even when the flames were licking the flesh from their bones, without that supreme faith which savored of divinity?

Who could ever enumerate the miracles which faith has wrought in human history? It was through faith that the greatest discoveries and inventions were made.

The sufferings, the sacrifices, the years of painful, heartbreaking waiting, which hundreds of inventors had to endure, are beyond all human comprehension. Their superhuman endurance was made possible simply because of their faith in their own power to achieve, their loyalty to a voice which spoke from the great within of them, a voice which others could not understand or appreciate.

It has always been just in proportion to man's loyalty to this voice, this faith which is the substance of things hoped for, the evidence of things not seen, the prophecy of possible reality, that he has succeeded in accomplishing great things. It has ever been this supreme faith which has, little by little, lifted the race from the Hottentot to the higher civilization of today.

We do not understand the nature of this marvelous faith at all. Those who have it in a remarkable degree simply follow it. They obey the voice as Joan of Arc obeyed her "voices," the God urge within them which always leads its follower to a goal which not only lifts him, but lifts the race with him to greater heights.

Mankind has climbed to its present height upon the steps of faith. But while there is only now and then one who is willing to follow the voice of his soul, the faith that calls to him to advance, especially if it leads through trials and hardships and all sorts of deprivations, that voice haunts us all. There is some discovery, some invention, some possible improvement for humanity prophesied in every human being. There is not one of us that cannot do something toward lifting the race a little higher, if we only obey the call of God!

The lack of self-confidence, of a vigorous faith in one's mission is a weak link in most lives. The most difficult thing in the world is to make human beings believe in their own bigness, the grandeur of their mission, in the sublimity of their possibilities; and the greatest service that can be rendered a human being is to help him to discover his possibilities, for this establishes his faith, inspires him to pursue his ambition.

When a man gets a glimpse of the enormous power locked up in his nature he will not doubt again. His faith is established; and he will never rest until he brings out the other half of himself which is waiting to help him fight his battles and to move on to higher planes of thought and life.

A soul-consuming faith has ever been the power which has moved things in the world, which has built up all of the great religions, the new philosophies. It has been the fundamental principle of all human development and of all great achievement.

Faith is emphasized more than almost any other thing all the way through the Bible. It was by faith that Abraham accomplished his marvelous work; it was by faith that Moses led the children of Israel through the Wilderness. All the prophets in the Old Testament are constantly emphasizing the power of faith; and Christ Himself, Paul and all the other great New and Old Testament writers were constantly emphasizing the miraculous power of faith to achieve, to accomplish.

How many times Christ said, "According to thy faith be it unto thee." Two words that He emphasized more than all others were faith and belief. These seemed to be magic words. They carried a tremendous force, more powerful than electricity. The Savior constantly reiterated the might of faith, the power of belief. "Be not afraid, only believe." "Be of good cheer; it is I, be not afraid."

"According to thy faith." This is the burden of His message to His chosen twelve.

And how often He had to reprove them for their lack of faith, their timidity, their fear, their unbelief! Again and again when they failed to accomplish that which He sent them out to do, He reproached them: "Why are ye so fearful? How is it that ye have no faith?"

He assured them that only on one condition could they do the work He was training them to do – that they have faith. Having this, they should do even greater things than He was doing. "Verily, verily, I say unto you, he that believeth on me, the works that I do shall he do also; and greater works than these shall he do; because I go unto my Father."

"Heal the sick," He urged, "cleanse the lepers, raise the dead, cast out devils; freely ye have received, freely give."

That something in human nature which, more than all else, reflects the divine in man, is faith. It is lack of it that causes many of the ills, much of time unhappiness, and most, if not all, of the failures in life.

If you lack this self-faith which is the sublime of man, if you are deficient in this great motor power which accomplishes things, which builds superb, masterful characters, you can make good your lack; you can supply your deficiency by daily auto-suggestive treatment for the acquisition or the strengthening of this greatest and most necessary of all human traits – faith. When giving a self-treatment, always get by yourself, and talk to yourself in a firm, decided tone of voice, just as if you were speaking earnestly to someone else whom you wished to impress with the great importance of what you were saying. Addressing yourself by name, say:

"You are a child of God, and the being He made was never intended for the sort of weak, negative life you are leading. God made you for success, not failure. He never made any one to be a failure. You are perverting the great object of your existence by giving way to these miserable doubts of yourself, of your ability to be what you desire with all your heart to be. You should be ashamed to go about among your fellows with a long, sad, dejected face, as though you were a misfit, as though there were not enough force in you, as though you had not the ability to do what the Creator sent you here to do. You were made to express what you long to express. Why not do this; why not stand and walk erect like a conqueror, instead of giving way to discouragement and doubt and carrying yourself like a failure? The image of your Creator is in you; you must bring it out and exhibit it to the world. Don't disgrace your Maker by violating His image, by being everything but the magnificent success He intended you to be."

There is a tremendous achievement force, an up building and strengthening power in self-assertion, in the asserting of the "I am." This is not egotism, not the glorification of the burlesque of the man or woman which wrong thinking or wrong living has made. It is simply the assertion of your kinship with the Father, a strong appeal in the first person to your other self, the ideal self, the self you feel you were intended by the Creator to be and which sometime, somewhere, you shall be.

But, remember, it is not enough to believe in yourself when you feel particularly happy, or when some good fortune has come to you. It is not enough to have faith spasmodically, to get enthusiastic over your prospects, and then undermine all your previous efforts by admitting doubt, fear, and discouragement to your mental kingdom. It won't do to keep dropping down again and again, like a frog trying to get out of a well, and feeling a little weaker and more discouraged after each fall.

Make it a habit to begin and end the day with a declaration of faith in yourself, faith in your God. Guard this faith continually as your most precious capital. Take no chances that this, your greatest life asset, shall be imperiled by weak, downhearted thoughts.

All doubts and fears, all pessimism and negative thinking poison the very source of life. They sap energy, enthusiasm, ambition, hope, and faith, everything that makes life strong, vital, and creative. Entertain only the mental friends of your ambition, those that will help you realize your ideal, that will help you to make your dreams come true, to match your vision with reality.

If you are grounded in faith, enemy thoughts will have no power over you, because your positive, affirmative mental attitude will bar them from your mind. You will be strong through the consciousness of the God within you, for "hereby we know that He abideth in us, by the Spirit which He hath given us." When a man realizes his kinship with the great creative Power, that he is in truth a son of God, he cannot be other than positive, forceful, radiant, self-reliant, a conqueror of that which would drag him back or hold him down. All the forces in the universe combine to help him to his goal.

The faith that we are God's children, gods in the making; the faith that we are a vital part of the great creative force of the universe; that we are a living part of the eternal God Himself will transform our lives.

6
FAITH AND DRUGS

"I AM the Lord thy God that healeth thee.

"I dress the wound, but God heals it." – Written by Ambrose Pare on the walls of the School of Medicine in Paris.

The potencies in the drug-stores are weaklings in comparison with the mighty life-giving, life-inspiring potencies which live in the great within of ourselves. It is here we make connection with the vital, creative, restorative power which first created us, and which recreates us, restores, repairs, and heals us.

To nothing else touching his life can the aphorism "As a man thinketh in his heart so is he" be more fittingly applied than to a man's health.

Health can be established only by thinking health, just as disease is established by thinking disease. Just as you must think success, expect it, visualize it, make your mind a huge success magnet to attract it if you are to attain it, so if you want to be healthy, you must think health, you must expect it, you must visualize it, you must attract it by making your mind a huge health magnet to attract more health, abundant health. As long as physical defects, weaknesses, or diseased conditions exist in the imagination, as long as the mind is filled with visions of ill health the body must correspond, because our bodies are but an extension of our thoughts, our minds objectified.

Health is based upon the ideal of the body's perfection and the absolute denial of disease, the denial of everything but the ideal condition; upon the idea that only that which is good for us can be real in the highest sense of the word; that all physical discords are only the absence of harmony, not the reality of our being, the truth of us. Health is the everlasting reality; disease is the absence of reality. It is only seeming in proportion to the physician's ability to suggest perfect soundness of body to his patient, to visualize him as physically perfect; in proportion to his power to see and to impress upon the mind of his patient the image of the ideal, instead of that of the diseased, discordant, suffering individual, will he be able to help him.

In 1866, Sir James Paget, who was then the most famous physician in England, in speaking of a case which had baffled him for a long time, told another physician that someday his patient would disgrace the profession "by being juggled out of her malady by some bold quack, who by mere force of assertion will give her the will to heal or forget or suppress all the turbulences of her marvelous system."

Many physicians admit that "quacks" often heal patients when the regular physicians can do nothing for them. But they do not realize the principle underneath this sort of healing by the "quacks," as they call them; that is, the power of assertion, the establishing in the mind of the patient the idea of his health, the wholeness of his body.

Whether we call him a quack, a healer, or a regular physician, he will help his patient best by acting on this principle, because the creative forces in the patient will all the time be building into the tissue of his body the reality of the perfect image, the image of the sound, robust being which the physician projects into his mind.

A great surgeon has told me that time and again he has performed make-believe surgical operations upon patients who had dwelt so long on the probability of disease in certain organs that they had become obsessed with fear and developed some of the symptoms of the disease.

In such cases as this the surgeon goes through all the forms of a regular operation. He puts the patient on the operating table, puts him under an anesthetic, and will sometimes scratch the skin so as to leave a little semblance of a trace of an operation. Then he will put a surgical bandage on the part and keep the patient in bed the usual time, at the end of which he is quite well again and perfectly normal.

Without exception, he says, all the patients he has treated in this way, whether for appendicitis or trouble in some other organ, have been entirely cured of their obsession. Even in cases where the patient had insisted that he had had persistent pain for many months have entire cures been made by a make-believe operation. Nor has this surgeon ever told his patients of the deception he practiced, which he claims was perfectly justifiable, because his great object was to help them get well with the least possible risk or harm.

Another surgeon in a large hospital says he has performed many such mock operations on hysterical women, who imagined they had some malignant growth or other cause for operation, after all other efforts to convince them that there was really nothing the matter with them had failed.

Among other cases be cured in this way was that of a woman who was convinced she had an internal tumor. She had been operated upon four times previously and had a tumor removed. Having received a severe shock from upsetting a lighted lamp, she became hysterical, and possessed with the illusion that she was again suffering from tumors and that the only thing that would save her life was an operation. Not being able to pacify her in any other way, the physician decided to perform a mock operation.

The patient was put on the operating table and given just enough anesthetic to put her in a state of semi-consciousness. She could bear and feel, but could not see. The surgeons and nurses moved about the room quietly, gave hurried orders to the attendants, and acted as though they were working on a grave operation. They let ice water drip from a considerable height upon the affected part for four or five minutes to give the patient the idea of being swathed in bandages. Later, she was taken home in an ambulance, and on awaking found two trained nurses creeping about her room. When asked if she could take a little sip of weak tea, she told the nurse that she felt frightfully weak and languid. But on being urged to make an effort, she succeeded in swallowing a little of the tea. The patient remained in bed ten days, after which her friends were allowed to see her and she gradually recovered strength.

Although there was no cutting whatever by the surgeon's knife, no real operation, this woman believed there had been, and the conviction of the relief it had afforded neutralized or destroyed the previous conviction that she was in a dangerous condition, and that nothing but an operation could possibly save her life.

A still more interesting case reported by the same surgeon was that of a young woman who kept moving her head from side to side constantly, telling her physician that there was a string in her head, pulling it this way and that. He could not persuade her that this was only a delusion, and finally sent her to a surgeon.

The surgeon decided to pretend to operate upon her, and when he told her that an operation was necessary, she clapped her hands for joy. She told him that other physicians and surgeons she had consulted only laughed at her and called her foolish while all the time she knew there was a string in her head and that she must be operated upon for its removal. The surgeon put her under an anesthetic, cut off some of her beautiful brown hair, and made a small skin incision, so she would think that the operation had been performed.

Then he took a section from an E string of a violin, soaked it until it looked like a cord or tissue, and when the patient recovered consciousness showed her this cord, saying he had removed it from her head, and that the operation was very successful. The girl immediately recovered. Nothing else could have convinced her, the surgeon said, that her head was not pulled constantly this way and that by a string, and she could get no relief until she believed that the string had been removed.

Now this make-believe surgical treatment is based on the same principle as the bread pill treatment, which has affected so many cures. It is wholly mental, and the cure is a matter of faith on the part of the patient, his belief in the efficacy of the remedy.

We all know that the benefits received from physicians and medicines or drugs depend upon faith, the patient's expectancy of relief, his belief that he is going to be cured. Destroy this faith and you kill the virtue of the remedy. Physicians well know that when a sick man's faith and hope are gone there is very little chance for his recovery. This is why they refrain as long as possible from telling a patient that there is no chance for him, because they know that this affects him as the death sentence affects a condemned criminal. It takes away hope, and thus destroys the only rallying force which can possibly tide the patient over a crisis. Every physician knows that courage, hope and expectation of a cure are powerful aids to healing. He counts upon these to supplement his specific treatment.

Expectancy of relief is literally of itself a powerful remedy. I have in mind the case of a man who had been suffering for years with a peculiar disease which no hospital treatment seemed able to reach. His hope of recovery was beginning to weaken when he heard of a foreign physician visiting this country who had built up a great reputation in the successful treatment of cases like his own. He read over and over in medical journals and newspapers of the marvelous cures affected by this physician until he had worked himself up into a perfect frenzy of belief that he also would be cured if he could only be treated by this wonder worker. Although comparatively poor, the cost meant nothing to him if he could only get relief from the torture he suffered. So great was his confidence that he was going to get relief that he mortgaged his home for every dollar he could get, and sold nearly everything else he had in the world in order to go to this great specialist.

When he reached the town where the specialist was he was obliged to remain some little time before he could meet him. But so profound was the man's faith in him that he was practically cured before he saw him or began to take his treatment. After an examination the specialist told him he was sure to get well, and even before the man had his prescription filled he felt complete relief from his trouble.

Just think of the tremendous psychological advantage in this case. The patient's mind was in perfect condition for receiving help from the doctor's treatment. He didn't have a doubt but that he was going to be cured, and he was cured – by his faith.

Many people have undoubtedly been cured of disease by their great faith in some worthless patent medicine. For a long time, perhaps, they believed that if they could only get that particular remedy they would be cured. Their expectancy was so great, their hope so large, and their faith so powerful, that when they realized the conditions which they believed would make them well they got the benefit of their optimistic thought.

For example, I know a very poor man who suffered tortures for many years with rheumatism. His joints and many parts of his body were so fearfully swollen that he was not only badly disfigured, but actually crippled. He had used all sorts of cheap remedies recommended by friends, but without any great hope or expectation of relief. But one day he read a very graphic account of the near-miracles which had been performed by some all-powerful patent remedy for rheumatism. It was quite expensive; however, something like two dollars a bottle, and two dollars was a small fortune to this poor man who could not work. There was no one to help him out but his wife, who earned their support by taking in washing, going out cleaning occasionally and picking up a little money in any way she could earn it. By dint of extra hard work she managed to save the price of a bottle of the wonderful remedy. For months the man had been dreaming about what it would do for him. He pictured himself as growing stronger and better after every spoonful from the precious bottle. When at last his wife succeeded in getting the medicine for him, it had precisely the effect he had pictured. What he expected, what he had anticipated, actually happened. Just think of a dead, inert drug which couldn't move itself even in a thousand years moving man, the mightiest power in the universe!

The virtue is not in the inert drug. The curative quality comes from the person's faith in it. Destroy faith in it and you destroy the virtue of the remedy. There must be faith in the physician or the sick person will get no benefit from his treatment. Faith must accompany the drug, the prescription, or it will be powerless and the cure will be in proportion to the faith. If the patient's mind is prejudiced in the very least against the physician, or if he fights against the remedy, this will counteract the influence that otherwise might be beneficial. The diseased cells in any part of the body can only be repaired by the creative energy, the life force in the cells themselves, and this must be stimulated by hope, faith, and expectancy of relief. It is powerfully reinforced by faith in a certain physician or a certain remedy.

We have proof of this in the fact that the same remedy may have a wonderful curative effect upon one patient who possesses great faith in the physician and the remedy, while the same thing will have no effect whatever upon another lacking faith but having a similar constitution and temperament, and suffering from exactly the same malady. In other words, under exactly the same circumstances, the same remedy will have a powerful effect when animated by faith, while it will have no effect whatever without faith.

While there is no denying the fact that the majority of people fill their medicine closets with all sorts of concoctions that work havoc in mind and body, it would be suicidal to condemn entirely the practice of medicine and the use of drugs and other physical remedies as long as the vast mass of the people believe in them, because their faith will help them. If the fixed belief of the race is that certain remedies will cure certain diseases, corresponding results will temporarily follow their use, for the body conforms to our faiths, our beliefs. But look back over medical history and see what ridiculous remedies the race has believed in. They had their day and perhaps served their purpose, but because the progress of the world has taken us far away from them, how superstitious and absurd they seem to us today.

It is not so long ago since thousands of men carried horse-chestnuts in their pockets, or wore iron rings to rid themselves of rheumatism. There have been hundreds of remedies for rheumatism, each one of which had its vogue and then passed away. The horse-chestnut and the iron ring enjoyed great popularity in their day and furnished relief to many rheumatic sufferers. Thousands of such devices which were once standard remedies for certain diseases seem ridiculous today even to the most ignorant. But when the faith of the people was fixed upon the idea that the particular charm carried on the person, or the inert drug put into the living organism, would recreate a diseased cell, or restore lost tissue, certain advantages naturally followed their faith.

The history of medicine is largely a history of the rise and decline of people's faith in different remedies. Tens of thousands of such remedies which have been used with good results in medical practice in the past are now obsolete because the faith of the physicians, the faith of the public have gone out of them. They were effective while people's faith in them continued, but when the faith they had inspired evaporated their virtue also evaporated. Everything depended upon the reputation of the remedy, upon the belief in its power.

A similar thing is true of popular physicians. Sick people want one of great reputation, one in whom everybody believes, and it is almost a universal experience that patients feel much better after the visit of such a physician, even before he has written a prescription or they have taken any of the medicine he advises. And every physician knows how common it is for ignorant patients to feel very much better just after taking a dose of prescribed medicine, long before it could possibly have gotten into the circulation or physically affected them. Physicians really owe their success largely to people's faith in them and their remedies.

Faith is at the bottom of all cures, at the bottom of all achievements, physical or mental.

Religious history is full of examples of people who have been cured of all sorts of diseases by going to famed miraculous springs, by bathing in sacred waters, or streams supposed to have great curative qualities.

A friend of mine when traveling in India went to the Ganges during a great pilgrimage, when multitudes of believers had gathered on the banks of the sacred river to bathe in its healing waters. He saw tens of thousands of these people, afflicted with different diseases and some with open sores, bathing at one time, and so close together that they could scarcely move. The water was absolutely filthy, and dead bodies were floating about in it, close to the bathers, and the bathers were actually drinking the sacred water!

Many of these poor wretches had come long distances on their hands and knees, from which the skin was worn off. They had looked forward so long to bathing in these sacred waters, had undergone such terrible sufferings and privation in order to reach them that they had built up a tremendous faith in their efficacy. So profound was their belief in their healing power that a great many of them were actually cured by the very waters which carried in them the germs of disease and death. Those waters which would have killed people who lacked faith in their virtue cured many of these poor ignorant, deluded pilgrims.

Our great watering-places, famous health resorts, and healing springs all have a similar history. The faith of the sufferers in all such instances works the apparent miracles.

I have witnessed the healing of numbers of sick people at the church of St. Jean Baptiste, in New York, at the annual novena of St. Anne. Here the agency which wrought the miracle was supposed to be part of the wrist bone of St. Anne. This relic was brought from a Canadian church in 1892, and every year since a novena in honor of St. Anne, which lasts for nine days, is celebrated at the church of St. Jean Baptiste. Throngs attend this novena, to receive the healing touch of the sacred bone, which is encased in silver and glass. All along the altar rails, inside of which is the shrine of St. Anne, people crowd together kneeling, while a priest, carrying the sacred relic, passes along and touches with it the afflicted part of each one of the faithful as indicated by the sufferer. This may be the head, the arm, the hand, the eye, the ear, but, whatever the part, the priest touches it quickly with the relic, at the same time uttering appropriate prayers. Marvelous cures are seemingly affected by contact with the relic, because this is the climax of the victims' faith.

It is well known that the incantations of the savages, the ceremonies of the Indian medicine men, and all of the many superstitious rites practiced by various peoples, have resulted in quite a large percentage of cures.

All of these things show that it is not the superstition, it is not the ceremony, it is not the relic, it is not the medicine, it is not the sacred water, but the faith that does the cure. This is the principle in all methods of healing, from those practiced by the lowest savage tribes to the highest civilization. The faith of the sufferer is the chief thing. Christ never said my faith, but thy faith hath made thee whole.

Faith in the shrine, faith in the remedy, in the superstition, in the physician, in the surgeon; faith in the hospital, faith in any and all methods of healing, – this is their potent virtue.

The Indian medicine man with all his grotesque and ridiculous incantations cures perhaps quite as large a percentage of diseases as does the average physician. Vast multitudes of people whom no medicine or material remedy could help have been cured at the various shrines which they sought at tremendous sacrifice to themselves, because of their profound faith, their absolute conviction that in this way and in this way only, could they be cured.

Faith is the sovereign remedy of the race. Faith is the builder, the creator, the restorer of life. Without faith we can do nothing. The Christ Himself constantly reminded His followers that without faith they could do nothing. Even He could do nothing for those who lacked faith. Does not the Bible tell us that in His own country, "He did not many mighty works there because of their unbelief?"

The benefit received by those who appealed to Him was always in proportion to their faith. It was always "According to thy faith be it unto thee." His words to the afflicted who came to Him for relief were "Believe ye that I can do this?" And when He had healed He claimed nothing for Himself, it was always "Thy faith hath made thee whole." In other words, He was always trying to arouse the faith of the people, trying to impress them with the tremendous power of faith, faith in God and in themselves, assuring them that faith, even as a grain of mustard seed would enable them to do marvels.

Christ never once referred to His own faith as to the quality which would enable Him to perform His supposed miracles. It was the faith of the people in His power to heal them that He emphasized. And just think what Christ's reputation for healing meant to the simple people of Galilee, the reputation of the Man who was performing such wonderful miracles – opening the eyes of the blind, making the lame to walk, the dumb to speak, the deaf to hear, curing the leper of his supposedly incurable disease, and even raising the dead to life! Think of what the rumors of such mighty doings would mean to such simple folk! Why, their faith in Him was unbounded.

Think of the mighty faith that moved people to let the sick down through the roof of houses in order to get them near this marvelous character? Is it any wonder that their diseases fled at His touch, nay, at His word? In view of all this does it seem strange, or unscientific that Christian Scientists, Mental Scientists, Divine Scientists, and others, believing in the power of God working through man, should perform such miracles of healing and of ability increasing by pure faith? And if the curative qualities of the remedies used by physicians are so largely due to faith in them, which physicians themselves acknowledge, why not leave out the drug and apply only the healing faith? Why not depend wholly upon faith, as Christ did, and as the mental healers do?

The homeopaths made one jump from enormous doses to almost nothing, with apparently the same results. The mental healers have simply taken one more step. They are depending wholly upon faith, and they seem to perform about as large a percentage of cures as the regular medical profession. And, as a rule, their cures are very much more permanent, because truth eradicates the roots of the disease, which many physicians now believe to be entirely mental.

Christ never once referred to any other healing principle than faith. It was always faith, and this is the principle on which all mental healing is based. The success of the mental healer depends upon his own faith and the faith which he is able to arouse in the patient. If there is no faith there is no cure. Some will say that many people are cured without faith, even against their will; but the very fact that these people seek treatment is proof that they do have faith or they wouldn't go to the healer. Of course the healer's faith has much to do with healing, but a real permanent cure can only be affected through the faith of the sufferer.

The healing principle is in the patient himself. The mental healer does not heal his patient. He merely arouses the divinity, the healing principle in the sufferer. Whether it is an allopath, a homeopath, or a mental healer who treats you when you are sick, it is always the God force in you that heals. It is the same force that created you and sustains you, the force that comes to your rescue in all your troubles, that same force which rushes to unite the broken bone, to heal the cut or wound, to repair the crushed tissue, to make you whole again. There is only one healing force and that is the creative force.

We hear a great deal about the healing principle of the divine mind, but it is the divine mind in you, and not outside of you, it is the divine principle inherent in your divine nature that does the healing. It is the creative principle which is everywhere in the great cosmic intelligence that heals all your hurts and restores you to health. This is the same creative principle which develops the germ in the acorn and carries it up to the giant oak; that develops a tiny germ into a beautiful full blown rose. It is this creative principle which is everywhere present in the universe, which inheres in every atom, which is, in fact, the reality of every atom in the universe, for the reality of everything is God.

The reality of ourselves, the truth of our being is God, otherwise we could not exist. It is no outside power which comes to our rescue, sustains us, holds us up, and guides us. It is the creative God power within us. This creative power is inherent in every cell of your body, in every particle of matter. This is the reality of us, the truth of our being. We literally live and move and have our being in God.

A realization of this truth, an ever-increasing consciousness of our oneness with the Supreme Power will bring ever-increasing peace and serenity of mind and health of body. An ever-increasing sense of our cosmic consciousness will increase our mental sense of well-being, of security, of safety from all that would injure us or destroy our happiness.

Someone has said that "to think of the presence and power of God as a healing life force, is to come in actual mental contact with that presence. To continue this thought by sturdy affirmation of healing truth will attune the mind to harmony with that beneficent power, lifting it out of the darkness and heaviness of mortal thinking into the brightness and joy that is the result of thinking God's thought after Him."

We do not realize the power of thought, because we do not appreciate the fact that we actually come in contact with whatever we think about or contemplate. This contact is no less real because it is mental; and it has power to influence the body, as well as the mind.

Never think of yourself as weak, diseased, sick, and deficient in any faculty, in any function. Think of yourself as perfect and immortal and your mind and body will tend to respond to this demand for wholeness and completeness.

The images of unfortunate symptoms, every sick or weak suggestion harbored in the mind are fatal to the realization of the ideal. Sick thoughts, weak, deficient thoughts, make a weak, deficient body and a crippled mentality. Think wholeness, think completeness regarding yourself. If you really believe that you are made in your Maker's image you cannot think too magnificently of yourself.

No matter how your body may seem to contradict this ideal of yourself, persist in holding it, and the weaknesses, the deficiencies and the discords which hinder your progress will gradually give way to the dominance of the divine image in you. The life processes within you will build the outward manifestation of this sublime image of yourself, and you will become normal, Godlike.

Many people who do not understand the science of mental healing think it is affirming what we know to be untrue, to persist that we are all right, when our bodies are racked with pain and we are really unable to work. But when we say we are well, even though we are suffering pain, we mean that the reality of us is well, that the truth of our being cannot be sick, cannot suffer, cannot know any discord, because that is divine.

You should always affirm the truth of your being, not its untruth, its error. Affirming your spiritual ideal always and everywhere will help you to grow into His likeness, into the likeness of perfection, while the contemplation of disease, the habit of looking at it as a reality, of regarding it as a truth, will tear down all of your physical building, will keep you constantly susceptible to disease.

You cannot build up a strong resisting body when you are constantly thinking of disease, concentrating on it, listening to its affirmation. Deny everything that is wrong, everything that is false, deny everything that is not God created and you will be all right.

But remember that merely denying is not destroying. You must not, as many do, deny in such a way as to make a stronger impression upon your mind of the thing you wish to get rid of. While denying the reality of sickness you must keep in mind the truth of its opposite, the spiritual ideal, and the spiritual man, which is never sick and never can be. Cling to the perfection ideal, the God ideal of yourself, no matter how loudly the opposite may scream, how busy it may be in asserting itself. The intelligence inherent in every cell in the body builds according to the model presented to it, and there is everything in holding up before the mind the perfect pattern, the health pattern, the health ideal.

Holding the ideal of health in the mind is the most scientific way of healing any physical discord or disease in any of the bodily organs, because the community cells themselves in any organ through their collective intelligence are powerfully influenced by the messages which come from the central station of the brain. These cells are very susceptible to encouragement or discouragement. They respond quickly to hope or despair, hence the tragedy of treating the body with discouragement.

All forms of mental healing are based upon suggestion of the divine ideal, and the healing is effective just in proportion as the mind of the sufferer is kept saturated, whether by autosuggestion or by daily help of the healer's mind, with the divine ideal, with the health principle of the divine mind.

The suggestion that health is the everlasting fact, and that disease, sickness are counterfeits, the absence of reality, is a healing force. Whatever form the mental healing process takes it is holding the ideal of wholeness, completeness, the thought that the sufferer is the child of divinity and that his birthright is health and wholeness that does the work.

When I hold the ideal of perfect health I do not picture or visualize the human side of myself. This may be a mere apology of the divine side of myself. I hold the ideal of the divine self, the perfect self, that part of me which was never born and which will never die, that part of me which was never sick or diseased, and which will never suffer defeat or disaster. This is the triumphant side of my life, the divine side, and this is the ideal which I shall always cling to. I shall cling to it because this is the pattern which I wish to build into my life, and I know that by holding this divine pattern, this divine ideal in my mind, it will be reproduced in my body.

On the other hand, if I hold the ideal which corresponds to the seemingly weak, defective or diseased part of myself, this inferior ideal will be built into my life, and all my standards will correspond to my lower ideal. If I constantly think and say to myself "I am physically weak, I have inherited unfortunate disease tendencies from my ancestors, who died with consumption, with cancer, with stomach trouble, with liver trouble or heart disease," I shall tend to realize these conditions.

You can never establish health except by thinking and affirming health principles. You must hold the health ideal. You must constantly and vigorously assert, "I am health; I am vigor; I have a robust constitution; I am power; I am perfect physically; the Creator never handicapped me by passing along to me the inherited weakness or disease tendency without putting in me a force which is more than a match for it, without giving me the ability to overcome my handicap. My health is based upon the consciousness of the truth of my being, the reality of me, the divine of me. It is based upon what I have inherited from my Maker; and this knows no disease, no weakness, no sickness, no deterioration, and no death. What I have inherited from my Maker is immortal, as He is immortal."

The famous Dr. Richard C. Cabot, of the Harvard Medical School says that the medical environment is most unfavorable to a patient's recovery. Sick people, who are steeped in the medical atmosphere, where they constantly hear the talk of disease symptoms, find it very difficult to get away from the sick thought. They are saturated with it when the mind ought to be filled with just the opposite. They should be in an atmosphere where everything around them will suggest health, instead of sickness and disease.

Some people unconsciously keep the body in a diseased condition by dwelling on disease. I recently heard of a woman who had been ill for a long time and who went to a mental healer for advice. She said she wanted to tell him frankly that although she had suffered a great deal, she didn't know whether or not it was God's will that she should get well, and she didn't know whether it would be quite right for her to take the chances of displeasing God by taking steps to get well!

Among other troubles, this woman had a tumor on her neck, and she insisted that the healer should see how very bad it was, for she said he couldn't possibly help her unless he knew all about it, her symptoms and all the details concerning the tumor. She had dwelt upon her troubles and defects so long that she was obsessed with them. She couldn't see or think of anything else.

When she came for her first treatment the healer had ready a large vase of beautiful California roses, which were about the color of a natural, healthy pink skin. He told her to sit down and look at them, to drink in beauty, and to think about their perfection. To put her mind in a better condition to receive a treatment he made her look at the roses for a half hour. He told her that he didn't want to hear anything about her troubles, because a healer must see only the person God made, the perfect, whole, complete being, with strong, robust health, otherwise he could not help anyone. He instructed her to hold the same thought; to hold in mind only the ideal which her Creator had of her, not to think of any blemish, weakness or disease.

The woman obeyed instructions, and under the influence of this dominant health thought, through the persistent holding of the health ideal, her tumor gradually grew smaller, shriveled up and all her troubles disappeared.

Such healings support the fact that the body is but objectified thought, and that when the thought is changed the body also must change. The habit of always thinking of ourselves, of every faculty and function, as complete, whole, as sublime, glorious, would gradually revolutionize our lives.

The time is rapidly coming when disease, sickness, will not be mentioned in the home; When all physical defects and weaknesses will be tabooed; when, instead of being saturated with illness and disease thoughts, children's lives will be permeated with the health thought, the thought of wholeness, of completeness, physical and mental vigor, beauty, grace; when joy, gladness, optimism will take the place of the old discouraged, sickness and disease thought and conversation in the home.

In the future we shall live up to the health ideal our Maker designed for us, because we shall hold the right thought about ourselves. Merely stopping our aches and pains and curing disease is not enough. To be merely well is not achieving the real health ideal. The man that God planned was intended for a very different quality of health.

It is the overflowing fountain, not the one that is half full or just full, that makes the valley below green and glad. It is abounding health, health that is bubbling over, superabundant energy that counts. This is the health that makes mere living a joy.

If you charge your whole nature with the health ideal, if you think health, dream health, talk health; if you believe that you are going to be strong and healthy, because this is your birthright, your very magnetism will be healing to others. You will be a living illustration of the power of divine mind over all sickness and disease.

7
HOW TO FIND ONESELF

FEW MEN find themselves before they die. – Ralph Waldo Emerson.

It's that bigger, grander man beating beneath the dwarf of a man you feel yourself to be that is important.

There is a legend that "when God was equipping man for his long life journey of exploration, the attendant good angel was about to add the gift of contentment and complete satisfaction. The Creator stayed his hand – "No," He said, "if you bestow that upon him you will rob him forever of all joy of self-discovery."

The greatest moment in any life is the moment of self-discovery, the moment that gives a human being the first illuminating glimpse of his divine powers, that moment which opens the door into the great within of himself and shows him his godlike possibilities. The greatest event in any life is that which arouses the God in him.

The principal of a New York evening high school, telling an interviewer how she had discovered herself, said:

"When I felt that there was need of me in the world, I awoke to the fact that there must be a soul in me, a something bigger than I was, and therefore a something that I must give to others. I have always believed in the school as a hitherto unrecognized field, because the world is a school, and the application is therefore limitless."

This teacher is remarkably successful because she discovered early in life that *something* bigger than herself, which she felt she "must give to others." Although educated as a society girl, the call from the within of herself to teach, was so loud that it could not be resisted. Through teaching she has not only found the larger woman in herself, but she is also helping thousands of other women and girls to do the same for themselves.

One of the most difficult things in the world is to get people to realize the extent of their latent powers, to believe in their own bigness, in their own possibilities. The reason is that they see only a part of themselves, because they have only partially discovered themselves.

"Each of us," said Professor William James, "has resources of which he does not dream." If we could only turn a spiritual X-ray on ourselves most of us would find powers and potencies in the great within of us which may not have gotten even to their germinating stage. There is probably not a living being who would not be amazed if he could see unfolded in panorama all of the potentialities within him, if he could only glimpse the man he might be. He would say, "These remarkable success qualities belong to someone who has achieved distinction, not to an unknown person like me."

All of the potencies and possibilities of a giant oak are wrapped up in the acorn, and under the right conditions they would unfold to the full in a perfect oak. When we see a scrub oak which has come from a perfect acorn, we know that it has been dwarfed by wrong conditions, that only a very small part of the possibilities infolded in the acorn were ever unfolded. The mean little scrub oak expresses only a fraction of the immense possibilities that lay buried in the parent acorn.

The same is true of every child born into the world. All of the latent forces, the powers and possibilities locked up in the human acorn under right conditions, would develop to full and complete expression in the ideal man or woman.

And this is what Nature, in all her work, is ever after, the ideal, the perfect specimen that reaches up to the possibilities foreshadowed in the seed. She is not after the dwarf oak; nor does she want the shriveled, blighted wheat that has been starved and stunted by uncongenial soil, by droughts, or other unfavorable conditions. It is the perfect wheat that was foreshadowed in the parent kernel she wants. Above all, it is the possible man, not the scrub oak or shriveled wheat variety of man that Nature is ever after. What you are is not a thousandth part as important as the ideal man, the possible man existing in the life germ within you.

It is only now and then that we see a giant human oak, where practically all of the possibilities of the acorn have been unfolded and given complete expression, as in a Socrates, a Gladstone, a Lincoln. Most of us are human dwarfs, scrub oak men and women, in whom only a minimum of the possibilities of the human acorn have found expression.

Yet I believe the time will come when the average man will be larger than the most magnificent specimens yet shown to the race.

What you are capable of being and doing is your greatest life asset. What you are actually doing may be a dwarfed thing compared with the giant achievement you are capable of. It is not what you have done, but what you long to do, what you feel capable of doing that will, if you struggle to express your ideal, count most.

Up to this time you may have been seriously hampered or dwarfed in your development. All sorts of things may have happened to the possible man, or the possible woman in you, to limit its growth, to restrict it, to impoverish it. But it is that superb thing that is possible to you, the thing which the Creator sent you here to do that you must strive to express. It is the man or the woman He wrapped up in the human acorn that you should struggle to evolve. It's that bigger, grander man beating beneath the dwarf of a man you feel yourself to be that is important.

In the great within of yourself there may be vast powers which you have never called out. Who can tell what unwritten books that would inspire, or set the world thinking, may be in your undiscovered reserves? Undeveloped beauty which would enchant men may be locked up inside of you, waiting for expression. What possible harmonies and melodies may be stifled, still silent in the octaves of your being! What masterfulness, what vast reserves of helpfulness, inspiration, and encouragement may still lie uncovered within you!

You doubt that there is anything of the kind? But you do not know. Many a man has carried locked up within himself for more than half a century the germs of a mighty genius without even guessing at it. There are multitudes of men and women all over the world who are as ignorant of their possibilities, of their hidden success assets, as the Native American Indians were of the resources of the great Western Continent when Columbus discovered it.

Emerson says, "Few men find themselves before they die." Very few people ever make exploring voyages within themselves, and they carry with them to their graves undiscovered confines of ability. The great majority die without developing their possible efficiency of hand, or tongue, or of brain; without developing any of the special gifts locked up in the great within of themselves. Most of us die with the great secret, with the sealed message which the Creator put in our hands at birth, still unread, because we have never learned how to open or how to read it.

Young men often say in excusing their lukewarm efforts, "If I only knew that I had the ability of a Roosevelt, an Elihu Root, a Wanamaker or a Marshall Field that I could stand at the head of my profession or business, there is no amount of hard work or drudgery I would not undertake. No matter how many years it might take, if I was sure of ultimate success, I would not mind the work or the time."

But how do you know, I ask? How can you be sure that you have not a lot of this ability you long for locked up in yourself? If you have not tried your strength, how do you know what you may be able to do? You may have more ability slumbering within you than you dream of. Why waste your precious time thinking about other people's genius? Why not unlock your own, see what you have, bring it out into the light and develop it? You may have something of a Roosevelt, something of a Marshall Field in yourself; you may have something very much greater than either of these men manifested waiting your help to give it expression.

When we know that even the great majority of men whom we call successful use only a comparatively small part of their ability because they never find all of themselves, why should any of us put a narrow limit to our possibilities, remain paupers in achievement when we might be princes?

We set our own limitations. Emerson hammers this truth home to all of us in his "Essay on Self-Reliance." He says: "That popular fable of the sot who was picked up dead drunk in the street, carried to the duke's house, washed, dressed and laid in the duke's bed, and, on his waking, treated with all obsequious ceremony like the duke, assured that he had been insane, owes its popularity to the fact that it symbolizes so well the state of man, who is in the world a sort of a sot, but now and then wakes up, exercises his reason and finds himself a true prince."

There are enough powers, enough resources in the minds of the people in the great failure army today to revolutionize the world if their sleeping potencies could be aroused; if they could only be made to believe in themselves. If they could only learn how to enter into the secret depths of their nature, to get hold of themselves, to arouse latent qualities and powers, they could do marvelous things.

The great problem is to know how to get at the force in the great within of ourselves and to put it to work to the best advantage. For whether life shall be a success or a failure depends upon the call we make on our resources, the extent to which we develop all our possibilities.

The other day I was trying to encourage a young man, who had the opportunity, to start out for himself, instead of settling down in a narrow groove to work for somebody else all his life. "I am afraid," he said, "I haven't the courage to take chances. I have always worked for somebody else. I have never made a program for myself; never started anything on my own responsibility. I don't dare to make the attempt lest I fail."

That young man will never get hold of half of his resources, because he is afraid to trust himself, afraid to branch out, to take chances. We don't know what we can do until we try, and unused faculties never grow or strengthen. Everywhere we see starved, stunted lives, people who have discovered but little bits of themselves, little patches cleared up here and there in the great wilderness of their possibilities. They couldn't believe in their inherent greatness. They couldn't realize that they were born into this world to do a certain work; and that to do that work they would need every bit of power they could develop.

The average youth starting out in life has no means of knowing what his total assets are. Our systems of education do not help him to discover his possibilities. He sees only the assets that lie on the surface, and if he is not instructed how to find those that are deep down below the surface, if he does not get into the right environment, if he does not make a call on the divinity within him, he may never develop the man it is possible for him to be.

Self-discovery is simply a question of finding God in ourselves; and this is just what the new philosophy helps us to do. This new philosophy is a trolley pole which connects us with the mighty current of infinite power, and then our life problems seem easy because we are not pushing our car ourselves. Infinite power does that.

Many people had never really met themselves until they became acquainted with this new philosophy. That is, they had never up to that time found the best part of themselves. They had previously been getting their living by their weak faculties instead of their strong ones. They had been in the position of people living in poverty on a little corner of their vast estate, ignorant that there were great deposits of undiscovered, unmined wealth.

The possibilities of mental expansion, enlargement of vision, quickening of the mental faculties, increasing the efficiency, – in other words, the possibilities of self-discovery in the new philosophy are almost unbelievable.

In the old thought one's ability is pent-up, shut in. Self-expression is stifled; one is hemmed in by race prejudices, race beliefs, race lies, by religious convictions, whereas in the new philosophy there is a freedom, a fullness of self-expression, which gives a feeling that one's latent powers are being unlocked and set free.

I have known of a case of this sort where a young man's ability seemed to be doubled and quadrupled in a very short time after he got into the practice of this new philosophy. Before that this young man said he was so hedged in by the old church traditions and prejudices, and by his great faith in drugs and patent medicines, to which he had been a slave, – his whole mentality was so blocked in and circumscribed, so narrowed, pinched, stifled by his old thought, that he could not seem to get any freedom of thought or expression.

This was due largely to the fact that he had been reared in a small town in the South where religious prejudice is very strong. In this town people brought up in one denomination believe that those in all the other denominations are doomed. This young fellow used to pity everybody who was not a Baptist because he felt sure that they were going to be damned forever. He had himself a perfect horror of committing the unpardonable sin, and he was filled with a slavish terror of death.

The new philosophy made him a different being, turned him around and opened up a new world to him. The things which had seemed so real and so tremendously important in the past have gradually faded into nothing, and he sees now that only the good is real. He realizes that if God is all, if there is no other power, if He made all that there is, everything must be good and only the good can be real.

This one principle together with the realization of the oneness of all life, the unity of all the things in the universe, has changed his outlook upon life, has unlocked his fettered faculties and given him a freedom of expression which he had never before dreamed possible.

We find ourselves in very different ways. Struggling with difficulties, disappointments, failures, great responsibilities, has been the means of recalling many human beings to themselves. "Returned with thanks," abusive criticisms have opened the door to fame to many an author, when if his first manuscripts had been accepted, his first book praised, he might have made a very indifferent author.

Ella Wheeler Wilcox at the beginning of her career sent out an article to nineteen different publishers before it was accepted. This has been the experience of many a great writer who, in his effort to overcome obstacles has found his larger self.

The greatest of their latent possibilities lies so deep in some natures that it takes the impact of a tremendous emergency, a great life, or national crisis to call it out. Any ordinary event, the easy way of prosperity, will not do it; it must be something which shakes them to the very center of their being and knocks out from under them every support. They must feel that they have nothing to lean upon but the creative power within – even the God who made them. So long as there is no supreme call made on the great within of them they never know their own resources. On the other hand the structure of many a divine success has risen out of the ashes of a burned fortune or apparently ruined hopes.

The San Francisco earthquake and fire was really the making of many lives. Thousands of men and women who had not amounted to anything before were suddenly brought to their senses, and to the discovery of their real selves. The crash which made such a terrifying rift in the earth for many miles, made a rift in their lives, uncovering vast assets which otherwise never would have been brought to light.

Like those plants which must be crushed before they will reveal their sweetest fragrance, or their beneficent properties, many people never reveal the sweetest thing in them until they are crushed by some great sorrow. They go through half a life or more unconscious of the richness which lies buried within them, when suddenly some great grief, some overwhelming misfortune reveals a wealth of personality, and of power which not even those who knew them best dreamed they possessed.

Job really never discovered his full power, his superb manhood, until he had lost all his material possessions; until the Bedouins had stolen his herds and burned his home, and he himself had been attacked with boils and all sorts of physical afflictions. But out of these terrible afflictions which tested his character came the light and strength which guided him to the haven of peace, a greater material prosperity and a higher manhood than before. It was only when overwhelming sorrows and losses had stripped him of his supposed friends, his family, and everything which he had thought worthwhile, and he was forced to depend upon God alone, that he really found himself.

The shock of the Civil War which uncovered the greater Abraham Lincoln also uncovered the greater Ulysses S. Grant. When he was forty years old, nobody outside of his own little community knew Grant. Up to that time he had not shown the slightest sign of what was locked up in him. No one ever dreamed there was anything remarkable in the man, and yet all of these years walking around unheeded among his fellows was one of the world's greatest warriors.

There was disguised in that apparently mediocre individual the man who next to Lincoln was to play the chief part in the saving of his country. There was locked up in that ordinary man one of the greatest military geniuses that ever lived. A quarter of a century of ordinary events and life routine did not even give a glimpse of the giant sleeping within him. He never dreamed what was inside of himself. Up to his thirty-ninth year or later everybody who knew Grant would have laughed at the idea (as he would have done himself) that he had ability to take any prominent part in the subduing of the great rebellion.

He was graduated twenty-first in a class of thirty-nine at West Point. At thirty-two he was a nobody, forced to resign from the army because of his great weakness. He went into the custom house, the real estate business, worked in a store, in a tannery, and was a comparative failure in them all. It was the supreme emergency of a war which threatened to disrupt the nation that revealed the real man to himself and to the world.

The late Justice Miller, who was for years regarded as the ablest man in the United States Supreme Court, told me that he did not even begin to study law until he was thirty-seven years old. He had not found himself until then. But in a little more than ten years from that time he was on the Supreme Court Bench.

Many people pass their fiftieth, even their sixtieth milestone, before they find themselves, before something happens which unlocks a new door in the great within of themselves and reveals new powers, new resources, of which they had never before been conscious. Then in a few years after their discovery they have redeemed half a lifetime of ineffectiveness.

We often hear men and women who have found themselves tell of the particular things which awakened their ambition; the accident, the sorrow, the emergency, the book, the suggestion, the encouraging friend, which first gave them a glimpse of their own possibilities, uncovered powers which they never before dreamed they possessed. If all of the people who have done things worthwhile in the world would only give an account of how they were awakened, tell of the things that had aroused their ambition, – the incident, the circumstance, the book, the lecture, the sermon, the advice, or the catastrophe, the failures, the crisis, the emergency, the afflictions, the losses in their lives, what a wonderful help it would be to the strugglers who are conscious that they have locked up within them forces which have not been aroused and which they cannot seem to get hold of.

The man who can write a book that will enable people to discover their unused assets will do an incalculable service to humanity.

Boosting from the outside will never help us to discover ourselves. We do our greatest work, uncover most of our latent power, when struggling to make good, when striving to make a place for ourselves in the world. Yet it is a strange fact that most people look not only for their pleasures but for all their personal resources outside of themselves. They go through life complaining that they have nobody to help them, that they have no chance such as many others have, excusing themselves for their failure or mediocre success on the plea that they lack capital, or "pull," or opportunity, when they have locked up right within themselves vast assets of untold value which they have never developed and which they never can use until they have found and made them available.

This is one reason why so many of the sons and daughters of inherited wealth discover so little of themselves. They go through life indifferently, carrying their great possibilities undeveloped to their graves, because there was no special motive for effort, apparently no necessity to exert even the surface power.

No son ever inherited wealth enough to uncover his greater possibilities. No father can do this for his son; it can be done only by self effort. Everyone who has ever made his mark on the world, who has done things worthwhile, has found his resources in himself.

The necessity for personal effort has made many a man famous, has compelled him to contribute to the uplift of humanity, to the progress of the world, who but for this priceless spur would have remained a practically useless member of society.

It is a most unfortunate thing for any boy to be coddled and waited upon until he has formed habits which make it very unlikely that he will ever exert himself sufficiently to arrive at the point of self-discovery.

A housewife explaining to her husband why the bread was not good said, "There is as good stuff in this loaf of bread as in any loaf I ever made, but nobody can eat it because there is not enough yeast in it. It did not rise."

This is just what is the matter with a lot of young people with good material in them, good man timber, good woman timber. They lack yeast. There is not enough of the rising quality, not enough of the yeast of a divine ambition in them to make them struggle to find and develop their highest power.

"Great masters are they who help you to find yourself," said Dr. Frank Crane. "The others simply find you."

There are a multitude of things which assist our self-discovery.

Keeping our minds in a positive, creative condition; keeping ourselves physically at the top of our condition, in perfect health; maintaining mental poise, a cheerful, happy mental attitude, by keeping our minds free from fear and worry and anxiety, – all of these things are great aids to self-discovery. And there is no secret about any of these things.

Self-confidence is a potent self-discoverer. Distrust, self-depreciation closes the doors to the locked-up potencies and powers within. Faith opens the door and releases them.

Seek every possible experience which seems to open up your nature and release new force. For instance, great lovers of music after listening to a wonderful voice, or going to an opera, feel something inside of them released, something which had been locked up before, something which they never really knew they possessed until then. Sometimes a great play will produce a similar effect upon people. They leave the theater feeling conscious of decided enlargement by the unlocking of latent forces within them. Our ideals are constantly being broadened and elevated by similar experiences.

A youth perhaps has slumbering in his nature great pent-up artistic or musical powers, but he has always lived back in the country, on a farm, where he never has come in contact with musical or artistic people, never has been thrown in a musical atmosphere. He never has heard music of any account outside of his little church choir, and remains quite ignorant of his latent possibilities until he goes to the city. There he hears famous musicians, great singers in concerts, in opera, and a new avenue is opened up in his nature, a new passion is aroused which sweeps away his farm ideals, and his plans for his career are instantly changed. He has discovered a new force in himself, which henceforth is to govern his life.

Here is another youth whose whole idea before he started for college was to go into the store, or some other business, with his father, but as he advanced in his studies, and the inspiration of the college professors pushed his horizon of ignorance a little farther and farther away, new forces were opened up and he made discoveries in his nature which completely changed his life aim.

Parents are often puzzled and troubled at what they think is the fickleness of their sons when they frequently change their ideas about their future careers. This is often because education unlocks new powers, opens up new possibilities to them, and changes their ideals and ambitions.

One of the great advantages of education and wide experience is that these help us to uncover more and more of our hidden powers. And these seem inexhaustible, for, no matter how many successive discoveries we make in ourselves, there apparently is no diminution of the remainder. In fact, human life seems to be a sort of a funnel. We pass into the small end at birth, and the farther we go the larger and larger grows the funnel. Our horizon keeps ever pushing out towards the Infinite, and there seems no limit to our possible growth.

Many people go through life without having their nature opened up to any great extent because they do not seek the occasions for growth. They do not take sufficient pains to get in an ambition-arousing, an ideal awakening environment.

Not long ago I wound my watch at night and in the morning I found that it had stopped. The hands were just where they had been when I wound it. I took it up; but the hands did not move. Then I gave it a violent shaking and it started at once and ran until the mainspring was exhausted the following night.

The power which enabled the watch to do what it was made to do was there all the time. All it needed was a little shaking up to start it going.

I have met many a youth who seemed to be standing still; there seemed to be no power engine inside of him to run his mental machinery effectively and while I was wondering when he would start up, his father, upon whom he was dependent, suddenly died or some other misfortune befell him. The jolt started his mental engine, and all at once he developed an amazing amount of energy and executive ability, which no one ever before dreamed he possessed. I have seen others whose road was made so smooth and easy for them that they never received sufficient jolting to set their mental engines working, and they have gone through life with the power still unlocked inside of them. On every hand we see even young men and young women standing still mentally and spiritually, making no progress toward further self-discovery.

They have ceased to grow.

Men and women who are trying to make the most of their lives, never stop growing. They are always on the road, because their goal is always receding as they grow larger, broader and more efficient. They only stop off at way stations to unpack a few things which they no longer need, impedimenta which hamper them, and then they resume their journey. This is the way all along the life path.

If you would get at your hidden resources, stimulate your growth and your power, you must be continually improving yourself somewhere; increasing your intelligence by closer and keener observation, by the constant study of men and things, the broadening of your mental and spiritual outlook, the getting away from self and the enlarging of your sphere of service and helpfulness.

Reading the world's great books – the Bible, Shakespeare, the life stories of great men and women, and association with noble souls are great helps to young people on their voyage of self-discovery.

Think of the secret chambers of possibilities which were unlocked in multitudes of people by men like Lincoln. There are thousands of people living today who are grander men and women, better husbands and wives, better lawyers, better physicians, better statesmen because of the example of Abraham Lincoln. The story of his life, of what he accomplished, opened up new avenues in their nature, our institutions are better, our civilization is higher because this grand man lived.

I know of no other means of self-discovery so potent as an inspiring book, and it is a great thing to keep such books near you, because ideals become dim if we do not constantly stimulate them by the right mental food. Listening to a great orator often stirs us to the very centers of our being, and awakens new impulses, new powers and determination in many a soul who up to that time had been asleep so far as knowing and utilizing his inner powers were concerned. Perhaps you have had this experience in listening to some great preacher or lecturer who seemed to open up a new world to you and give you a glimpse of realms in your nature which otherwise might have remained forever hidden.

"Man becomes greater in proportion as he learns to know himself and his faculty." The more highly we cultivate all our faculties, the more deeply we draw upon our resources, the more of our hidden selves we discover, the wider grows our vision. Life becomes a perpetual progress.

It has been a long journey up through the ages from the brute to the man, and on the way up we have developed such marvelous powers and resources as our primitive ancestors never dreamed of. Yet civilized man is still farther away from his ultimate destination, the end of the path of ascent, than he now is from the crude savage of his earlier stages.

Garrett P. Serviss says, "The human brain is only in its infancy, and since we are aware of that, we have good reason to hope that in the future web shall not merely know that the earth is full of power, but shall make that power, in some way, serve our uses."

We are all in a continuous process of development, and, as yet, strangers to the immense possibilities that sleep in the great within of ourselves. Uncovering these possibilities, finding our resources, should be the great object of every human being.

The wisest thought of the seven wise men of Greece was expressed in the two words carved over the entrance of the great Delphic Temple: "Know Thyself!"

"Know thyself!" This is really the chief business of man – to learn to know himself, to realize the power that is his through his inseparable union with his Creator.

8
HOW TO ATTRACT PROSPERITY

FEARS AND doubts repel prosperity.

Abundance cannot get to a person who holds such a mental attitude. Things that are unlike in the mental realm repel one another. Trying to become prosperous while always talking poverty, thinking poverty, dreading it, predicting that you will always be poor, is like trying to cure disease by always thinking about it, picturing it, visualizing it, believing that you are always going to be sick, that you never can be cured.

Nothing can attract prosperity but that which has an affinity for it, the prosperous thought, the prosperous conviction, the prosperity faith, the prosperity ambition.

Opulence follows a law as strict as that of mathematics. If we obey the law we get the opulent flow. If we disobey the law, we cut off the flow. Most of us tap the great life supply by inserting a half-inch pipe, and then pinch even this with our doubts, fears and uncertainties. There is no lack in Him in whom all fullness lies. The pinching, the limitation is in ourselves, "for He satisfieth the longing soul and filleth the hungry soul with good things."

We must conquer inward poverty before we can conquer outward poverty. True prosperity is the inward consciousness of spiritual opulence, wholeness, completeness; we cannot feel poor when we are conscious of being enveloped in the all-supply, that God is our partner, our Shepherd, and that we cannot want.

A poor woman who had all her life previously lived in the back country, moved to a progressive little village where, to her great surprise, she found that her new home was lighted by electricity. She knew nothing about electricity, had never even seen an electric light before, and the little eight-candle power electric bulbs with which the house was fitted seemed very marvelous to her.

Later, a man came along, one day, selling a new kind of electric bulb, and asked the woman to allow him to replace one of her small bulbs with one of his new style sixty candle power bulbs just to show her what it would do. She consented, and when the electricity was turned on she stood transfixed. It seemed to her nothing short of magic that such a little bulb could give so wonderful a light, almost like that of sunlight. She never dreamed that the source of the new flood of illumination had been there all the time and that the enormously increased light came from the same current which had been feeding her little eight candle bulb.

We smile at the ignorance of this poor woman, but the majority of us are far more ignorant of our own power than she was of the power of the electric current. We go through life using a little eight candle power bulb, believing we are getting all the power that can come to us, all that we can express or that destiny will give us, believing that we are limited to eight candle power bulbs.

We never dream that an infinite current, a current in which we are perpetually bathed would flood our lives with light, with a light inconceivably brilliant and beautiful, if we would only put on a larger bulb, make a larger connection with the infinite supply current. The supply wire we are using is so tiny that only a little of the great current can flow through, only a few candle power, when there are millions flowing past our very door. An unlimited supply of this infinite current is ours for the taking, ours for the expressing.

Multitudes of human beings go through life just as ignorant as was the poor country woman of the fact that there is unlimited light and unlimited power flowing right past their doors ready for their use, and that they may use all of it they can express. They are getting no more from the vast resources at their command than this woman was getting from the electric current. They seem to think that if they are expressing four candles, or eight candles power, that it is all the infinite supply can give them, or all that they were intended to have. It never occurs to them that the trouble is not in the current itself, but in the small bulbs they are using.

Millions have died in mental and physical penury, died weaklings, when they had within their own nature's vast possibilities of wealth and power which were never utilized, because they did not connect with the source which would have enabled them to express wealth and power.

Most of us strangle our supply by our pinching thoughts, our stingy, poverty thought, our doubt and fear thoughts. We pinch or entirely cut off the inflow of prosperity by our poverty-stricken mental attitude.

The stream of plenty flows toward the open mind, the expectant mind. It flows toward faith and confidence and away from doubt. It will not flow toward a stingy, pessimistic unbelieving mind, a fearing, worrying, anxious mind. We must keep the current open or the supply will be cut off. We cannot get a sixty or a hundred candle power supply through a four or eight candle power bulb.

The stream of plenty, of unlimited opulence, is flowing right past your door, carrying an infinite, never-ending supply of all the good things that heart could wish for. If you have the faith that creates, the faith that believes the best is coming to you, you can reach out mentally into this great stream of plenty – the universal supply – and get material aid to build what you will. The supply is there. It rests with you to make the connection that will draw it to you.

If all of the poverty-stricken people in the world today would quit thinking of poverty, quit dwelling on it, worrying about it and fearing it; if they would wipe the poverty thought out of their minds, if they would cut off mentally all relations with poverty and substitute the opulent thought, the prosperity thought, the mental attitude that faces toward prosperity, they would soon begin to change conditions. It is the dwelling on the thing, fearing it, the worrying about it, the anxiety about it, and the terror of it that attracts us to it and attracts it to us. We cut off our supply current and establish relations with want, with poverty stricken conditions.

Many people who have become interested in the new philosophy are greatly disappointed that they are not making any appreciable demonstration over poverty, that they are not advancing their position in life, not improving their conditions as they had expected they would.

Now, my friend, the law of abundance, of opulence, is as definite as the law of gravitation, and works just as unerringly. If you are not demonstrating as you expected to, you are probably still held under the bond of mental limitation, for there is no lack in "Him in whom all fullness lies." There is no limitation in the all-supply. The trouble is you try to tap it with a miserable little half or quarter inch pipe instead of a great big one, and the supply cannot flow through and flood your life with abundance.

If you pinch your supply pipe with your doubts and fears, your anxiety, the terror of coming to want, if you do not believe you can demonstrate abundance, you will get but a meager, limited supply instead of the inexhaustible flow you might have. In other words, the supply pipe is pinched only by your own mental limitations. By your doubts and fears and worries and unbelief, you can cut off all the supply and starve or, by a great magnetizing faith, a superb confidence in the all-supply, you can flood your life with all good things.

The law of supply is scientific. It will not act unless all the necessary conditions are fulfilled. Simply believing in the new philosophy and still keeping your old life doubts and fear habits, living in your old thought habits of lack and poverty, inefficiency, will not bring success. If you don't believe you will prosper and you don't practice what you believe, you will get no results. If you would reap its fruits you must obey the law of supply, the law of abundance, the law of prosperity.

Prosperity never comes by merely wishing or longing for it. Keeping your mind fixed on it, simply thinking of prosperity will never bring it to you. This is only the first step. You must cling to your prosperity thought, your prosperity ideal, but you must also back it up with scientific methods, the practical common-sense methods which all successful men employ in their work. You might dream of abundance and prosperity all your lifetime and die in the poorhouse, if you did not back up your dream with businesslike efficiency methods. That is, you must be methodical, orderly, systematic, accurate, thorough, and industrious. You must do everything to a finish. You must fling your energy, your heart into your business, your profession, your work, whatever it is.

One of the worst things about poverty is that it induces the habit of expecting poverty and failure, the habit of being half reconciled to its necessity.

No matter how poor you may be, if you have the right mental attitude you will not long remain poor. If you are determined to turn your back upon poverty and face toward prosperity, however your actual conditions may contradict this; if you really believe that you are a child of the Creator and Possessor of all things, that you were not intended for poverty, but that on the contrary the good things, the beautiful things of life are for you, the life glorious and not the pauper or the drudge life, you at once open your mind to the inflow of the prosperity current.

Have you, who are beating against the iron bars of poverty, ever stopped to think what marvelous things the Creator has everywhere provided for us His children? Just imagine the entire universe, the great cosmic ocean of creative intelligence, packed with all the riches, all the glorious things, the magnificent possibilities the human mind can conceive, and then try to picture what it would mean to you and to all who are complaining of lack and want if by some magic they could call out of this universal supply of creative intelligence anything which would match their desires, their heart longings. Imagine this vast universe, this ocean of creative energy, packed with possibilities from which human beings could draw everything which the wildest imagination could conceive, everything they desire in life, everything they need for comfort and convenience, even luxuries, – also cities, railroads, telegraphs and all sorts of wonderful inventions and discoveries. You will say, doubtless, that such a thing is too silly to contemplate for a moment. Yet, haven't human beings been doing this very thing since the dawn of civilization, all up through the ages?

Every discovery, every invention, every improvement, every facility, every home, every building, every city, every railroad, every ship, everything that man has created for our use and benefit he has fashioned out of this vast invisible cosmic ocean of intelligence by thought force. Everything we use, everything we have, every achievement of man is preceded by a mental vision, a plan. Everything man has accomplished on this earth is a result of a desire, has been preceded by a mental picture of it. Everything he has produced on this plane of existence has been drawn out of this invisible ocean of divine intelligence by his thought force. His imagination first pictured the thing he wanted to do; he kept visualizing this mental conception, never stopped thinking, creating, until his efforts to match his visions with their realities drew to him the thing he had concentrated on.

We all imagine that we actually, of ourselves, create these things. We do not. We simply work in unison with the Creator, and draw them out of the vast invisible cosmic ocean of supply. But we must do our part or there will be no realization for us. Just as the first step in an architect's building is his plan, so must we first make a plan or picture of the thing we desire. The architect first sees in all its details in his mind's eye the building to be erected even before he draws his plan on paper. He mentally sees the real building long before there are any materials on the spot for its construction. His plan has come out of the invisible, out of the fathomless ocean of possibilities which surrounds us. All of our wants and desires can find their fulfillment in this unlimited supply.

This is a marvelous revelation to man, the significance of which most of us have not grasped. Only here and there is there one who utilizes it in his daily living. But science is recognizing it. Edison says all scientists feel that "about and through everything there is the play of an Eternal Mind." They are recognizing that this is the first great Cause.

It is difficult to realize that every instant, under the impulse of Eternal Mind, miracles are leaping out from the cosmic ocean of energy into objectivity to meet our wants, to supply all our needs. Most of us are not able to grasp the idea that there is wealth and beauty and unthinkable luxuries waiting here for God's children. And because of this we do not materialize the things we desire.

It is one of the most marvelous things, in this wonderful plan of creation, that we actually live, move and have our being in this invisible ocean of limitless creative material, and that all we have to do to attract what we want is to hold the right mental attitude toward it and do our best on the physical plane to match it with its reality. Noah might have lighted the Ark had he known enough. The force was there just as today. When we once get it firmly fixed in our minds that in this invisible world of possibilities is everything which matches every legitimate desire and ambition, and that our own will come to us if we visualize it intensely enough, persistently enough, and do our best to make it real, we will no longer live in poverty and misery.

If you want to get away from poverty, if you wish to demonstrate abundance, prosperity, you must form the habit of mentally living in abundance; live in the ideal of what you want; that is, you must live the prosperity thought, you must hold the thought of abundance. Saturate yourself with it. Then the poverty thought cannot touch you. It will be neutralized because you cannot hold in your mind two opposite thoughts at the same time, and whatever thought you hold is a real creative force.

The great majority of poor people are poor thinkers, poor planners, and poor executives. They do not think prosperity, they do not obey the law of opulence, and so they stay poor in the midst of abundance.

You can no more attain opulence while holding the opposite thought than a youth could become a great lawyer by concentrating upon something else, thinking of other things all the time. The specialist makes his mind a magnet to attract the thing he is trying to attain. He dwells upon it, thinks of it, bends all his energies toward it, dreams it, lives it; and eventually draws it to him. In the same way, opulence, prosperity, obeys the law of attraction.

The idea of opulence must be implanted firmly in the subconscious mind, just as everything else which we desire to bring about, to draw out of the universal supply, must be impressed upon the subconscious mind by registering our vow, our determination there until it has become a fixed motive or actuating principle. Then it becomes an active influence in the life, an ever-increasing mental magnet that attracts the thing desired. Whatever we wish to bring about in the actual, we must first establish in the subconscious mind by a constant, positive, affirmative attitude toward that thing.

It is because they understand the importance, the imperative necessity, of this holding of the right mental attitude, that there is such a tremendous difference between the poverty of people who have imbibed the new philosophy and those who are still in the old thought. It is the difference between poverty with hope, poverty with courage, poverty with the expectation of something better coming, backed by a faithful effort to improve one's condition, and the poverty which is accompanied by despair, the poverty that has no hope for the future, the poverty that expects nothing better, that looks forward only to more and probably worse poverty, more pinching, more want and suffering.

Even the poverty with hope and expectation of better things is not a very comfortable state, but there is no despair in it, there is no real pain in it, there is not much real distress, because hope sees the goal beyond the blackness, it gives a light that dispels the gloom of limitation by showing a vista of good things in process of realization. It is the poverty which is accompanied by despair, which sees no light ahead and forces men and women to drudge on day after day without prospect of relief or hope of betterment that grinds the life out of its victims. This is the poverty that kills the spirit that destroys the buoyancy of life, the gladness and the joy, which are the birthright of every human being.

The poverty of those who have seen the light, who have gotten a glimpse of something better, the poverty which sees something ahead to work for, may be compared with the temporary discomforts which a family camping out for the summer may have to put up with. Knowing that their discomforts are temporary they make light of them. They do not impair their happiness, because they know conditions will soon change. They do not worry about their situation as they would if it were permanent and could not be remedied.

There are multitudes of ignorant, undeveloped people who are like many of the squatters on the desert in the arid lands of the West. These squatters build shanties and cultivate little patches around them, raising a few domestic animals to help them eke out a living. They barely exist, and yet the very soil from which they hardly get a living is rich with vast potencies, possibilities of bounteous harvests and the production of great wealth. If these people knew enough to mix brains with the soil, or if they would only settle somewhere near a supply of water so that they could irrigate their farms, they might live in luxury.

There is nothing lacking in the land, but it must have water and intelligence to develop its resources. These would make the desert fruitful. Water and intelligence mixed with the soil would perform miracles of cultivation where ignorance succeeds in producing scarcely enough to support a miserable existence.

Not far from such ignorant squatters I have seen a portion of the same desert land enriched by water and intelligent cultivation until it had become a veritable Eden of delicious fruits, vegetables, grains and flowers. Large families were living comfortably on an incredibly small piece of land, whereas before the introduction of water they would have half-starved on perhaps a hundred acres.

Most human beings live all their lives on deserts which are teeming with marvelous potencies and possibilities, but for lack of knowledge they live in poverty. Their mental resources yield nothing because they have not yet been developed. Some of us get a little irrigation into a corner of our lives and raise a few vegetables. Some of us cultivate a few flowers, and now and then one will get water and inspiration and ambition enough upon a little larger section of his mental desert and produce something worthwhile. But very few human beings ever cultivate their entire resources.

The new philosophy teaches us how to get hold of our resources, and how to use them, so as to get just what we want. It teaches us that the source from which all things spring is in the great cosmic intelligence which fills all space, and that in this vast cosmic ocean riches inconceivable are waiting to be objectified and utilized by man. It teaches us that all these things will respond to the right thought, the right motive, and that we can call out everything we desire from this All Supply. It holds that the reason why our lives are so lean, so pinched and poor, why our achievement is so limited, so picayune, in comparison with what we are capable of, is because we do not draw upon the All Supply.

Our narrow, limited, dwarfed ideals, our poverty-stricken view of things, the limitations our own thought imposes – these are the things that rob us of power and keep us in poverty. Our achievements or our possessions can never outrun our convictions or our ideals. We fix our own limitations.

When a man gets lost in the woods he cannot tell the direction in which he is facing, because he has lost the points of the compass. Unless a man so lost can see the sun and recover his bearings, he will walk around in a circle, thinking he is going in a straight line in a certain direction.

He makes no advance because he isn't facing toward his goal. He doesn't know this, but after a while when he finds he is not getting toward any opening and doesn't know how long he may wander about in a circle, he gets discouraged. Millions of people are lost in the dense woods of wrong thought. They are not traveling toward the goal of prosperity. They see no light, no way out of the woods, and they lose courage. They are turned about mentally, and don't know it.

If the people in the great failure army today could only be given prosperity treatments and shown that they are in their present predicament because of their wrong mental attitude, because they have been working for one thing and expecting something else; if they could only be turned squarely about so that they would face the goal of their desire instead of turning their backs upon it mentally, an enormous number of them would even yet make a splendid success of their lives. That is all that millions of people who are comparative failures in life, as well as the complete "down and outs," need to be turned about so that they would face life in the right direction.

What a pity it is that in this land of opportunity and plenty our Government should not have institutions conducted by experts for the treatment of poverty sufferers, those who are obsessed with the idea that their poverty is unavoidable. These people are just as much in need of prosperity treatments as the patients in hospitals are in need of health treatments. Most of them are curable. They have only lost their way on the life path and are facing the darkness instead of the light, facing towards the poverty goal instead of the prosperity goal. Their mental attitude needs changing so it will point toward success instead of toward failure, toward comfort and plenty, opulence, instead of poverty and limitation. Mental prosperity treatments would kindle a new hope in their discouraged minds, and expectancy of good things would take the place of despair. A new light would come into the eyes of those poor people; and if these prosperity treatments were administered to poverty sufferers in every country of the globe the world would take on a different appearance.

The time is coming when the State will have trained specialists, experts in the law of mental opulence, to give such treatments to the men and women who are in the great failure army, those who are headed in the wrong direction, those who have lost their way on the life path. But there is no need for those now suffering from poverty to wait for the coming of that time to be cured. Any intelligent person can apply the law and treat himself for prosperity.

Mental laws are clear and simple. We know that the fear thought attracts more fear, the worry thought more worry, the anxious thought more anxiety, the hatred thought more hatred, the jealous thought more jealousy, and the poverty thought more poverty. This is the law of attraction. Like every other law, it is unalterable.

The poverty disease can be cured only by its antidote – the prosperity thought. You carry within you this antidote to the poison of poverty, of lack, of pinching, dwarfing limitation. Use it, and cure yourself. The prosperity thought will kill the poverty germ.

Keep your supply pipes open between yourself and the infinite source of all supply. Don't pinch them by doubt, don't cut off the supply by limiting, pinching, poverty, lack thought. Keep your supply pipes wide open by the consciousness of your oneness with the One, your connection with the All Supply.

Abundance follows a law as exact as that of the law of mathematics. If we obey it we get the flow. If we pinch it, strangle it, we cut off the supply. Suppose a youth who had decided to study medicine and become a doctor should say to himself: "I cannot picture myself as a success because I don't know anything about what may come to me. Perhaps I haven't the qualifications that make a successful physician. I may never become one. I may be a failure. I doubt if I am fitted for it, but I'll try, anyway." Do you think such a timid, doubting, negative attitude would ever carry anyone to the success goal? Of course it wouldn't. The young medical student who is going to succeed is the one who pictures himself constantly as a successful physician, sees himself in a fine office, with a lucrative practice, climbing to the top of his profession. He is constantly visualizing himself as a successful physician.

Now, the same rule applies to the poor man who wants to become prosperous. He must picture himself as prosperous, he must obey the law of opulence by holding the ideal of opulence in his mind, and he must saturate himself with the prosperity thought, the thought of abundance.

If you wish to cure yourself of the poverty disease you should begin by giving yourself prosperity treatments something like this. Say to yourself, "If I am God's child I have inherited all the good things of the universe. I am heir to all supply, to the all-good. Poverty cannot touch the reality of me any more than disease can, for the reality of me is health. Health is the everlasting fact, and disease, sickness, is merely the absence of the reality.

Poverty is not my normal condition. There can be no lack, no poverty for God's image. 'All that my Father hath is mine.'"

Repeat daily the twenty-third psalm: "The Lord is my shepherd, I shall not want. He maketh me to lie down in green pastures; he leadeth me beside the still waters," etc. Follow this during the day with frequent assertions of your kinship with the Creator of all the universe. Commit these lines by Ella Wheeler Wilcox to memory, and frequently say them to yourself, vigorously, and with the force of absolute conviction:

"I am success. Though hungry, cold, ill-clad, I wander for a while, and I smile and say: 'It is but for a time. I shall be glad tomorrow, for good fortune comes my way. God is my Father. He has wealth untold; His wealth is mine, health, happiness and gold.'"

All the good things you need are yours by inheritance. Claim them, expect them, work for them, believe they are already yours, and you will realize them in your life. If you continually assert your kinship with God your Father, to whom all things belong, and send out the vigorous thought of abundance, a generous supply of all you need – which is your birthright – poverty cannot hold you its slave.

I was recently talking with a man who only a few years ago was so poor that he and his wife and children were reduced to a diet of bread and crackers without butter. They couldn't pay even the cheapest rent or buy themselves comfortable clothing. In fact, they were rapidly heading toward the ranks of the "down and outs." Today they are living in luxury, in a sumptuous hotel. They own a beautiful car, and have all they need to make life comfortable. They do not appear like the same people who but a comparatively short time ago were in a condition of semi-starvation.

Whence the change? Did someone leave them a fortune, or did they find a gold mine? No, nothing of that sort at all. They simply realized that their poverty was of their own making, that the cause of their miserable condition was entirely mental. And there and then they turned their backs on their despair environment and resolved that, no matter what appearances were, they would face the light and struggle toward it. As a result they began in a very short time to attract better things.

The whole family has now taken a new lease of life. The expression of despair and misery has gone out of their faces, and is replaced by the light of hope and joy. There is just the difference in their appearance and condition between despair and gladness, between the hope and expectation of more of the good things which belong to them, and the fear of want, the misery of grinding limitations.

Psychology is teaching us that all forms of discouragement, despondent thoughts, thoughts of doubt, of fear, of worry, must be kept out of the mind, for it cannot create while these enemies are in possession of the mental kingdom.

We are finding that in order to create, to build, we must hold a constructive mental attitude all the time, that we must keep all negatives, all thoughts of discouragement, despondency, of possible failure out of the mind. We are learning through psychology that we can produce only that which we concentrate upon, that which we constantly think of; that only that which is dominant in our mind, whether it is beneficial or injurious will be reproduced in our lives.

Your mental attitude will lead you into the light or hold you in darkness. It will lead you to hope or despair, to a glorious success or a miserable failure, and it is entirely within your own power to choose which it shall be.

Successful people, without knowing it, perhaps, are constantly giving themselves prosperity treatments, success treatments, by encouraging themselves, by making their minds positive, so that they will be immune from all negative, discouraging, poverty thought currents. Holding the success thought, the prosperity ideal, constantly dwelling upon one's successful future, expecting it, working for it, – these are, whether you know it or not, success, prosperity treatments.

Take, for example, men like Charles M. Schwab. Ever since Mr. Schwab was a poor boy starting in life he has been giving himself success treatments. He has held the ideal of prosperity, the vigorous, robust determination to be successful, to be prosperous. He has always faced the prosperity goal. If he had allowed himself to yield to the many discouragements he has had he never would have been the world's greatest steel master today, perhaps the greatest that ever lived. But he always triumphed over these negative, destructive, discouraging thoughts, by insisting on holding to the prosperity, the success, ideal.

Suppose that every little while Mr. Schwab should stop holding the success ideal and should indulge in discouraging, despondent thoughts, allow himself to get down in the dumps and feel that good fortune was deserting him, what do you think the result would be? Why, he would probably lose more in a single day by such negative treatments than he could neutralize in a week of prosperity treatments.

Every time you indulge in discouraging and gloomy, despondent thoughts, every time you allow yourself to get down in the dumps or in the blues, you are tearing down what you have been trying to build up by your success treatments, by holding the prosperous thought. Your attitude is hostile to prosperity, and your very atmosphere blights and strangles it. You practically say, "I long to have you, Mr. Prosperity, but I don't believe I ever will. You were evidently not intended for me, for everything I do ends in failure. There must be some strange fate that is keeping me from the success and prosperity I want. I really never expect to be prosperous, although I am working hard to get you, Mr. Prosperity."

It is such a mental attitude as this that is driving prosperity away from multitudes of people. If you want to better your condition you must get away from the conviction of poverty, you must keep the want thought, the poverty thought and conviction out of your mind; for these connect you all the time with the poverty and the lack thought currents from other like minds.

Multitudes of people through ignorance of the law condemn themselves to lives of poverty. They do not realize that, every time they think or say that they never expect to get away from the clutches of want, that no matter how hard they work there is nothing but the everlasting drudgery, grind and poverty for them, that fate is against them and they are doomed to remain poor, they are confirming and strengthening poverty conditions.

If we are ever going to enjoy abundance, we must talk abundance and freedom, not poverty and limitation. We must think abundance and not dam the stream of our supply so that we will get little drizzles instead of a generous flow.

What would you think of a prince who should go away from his father's palace and live in a poverty-stricken environment, in the midst of lack and want, and who should constantly claim that he couldn't do any better, that this was what was intended for him? You would say that it was his own fault; that there was plenty in his father's house and that it was his any time he chose to claim it; that the fatted calf and the royal robe were always waiting for him.

Yet most of us act just as foolishly. There is plenty of everything waiting for you in the All-Supply in our Father's house. It is yours by right of inheritance. Why don't you claim it? You cannot get it until you do claim it, any more than the prodigal son could enjoy his father's bounty while he continued to put it from him and feed instead on the husks of swine.

Prosperity, or opulence, in the larger sense in which we use it, is everything that is good for us, an abundance of all that is beautiful, uplifting and inspiring in life. It is everything that will enrich the personality, the experience, the spiritual life.

This opulence, which includes everything we can desire, is intended for all God's children. All we have to do to participate in it is to reach out into the cosmic intelligence with our thought, with our ideals, our aspirations and attract our own.

9
THINKING ALL OVER

> **EVERY CELL in us thinks. – Thomas A. Edison.**
>
> **Each cell in the body is a conscious intelligent being. – Professor Nels Quevil.**

Modern science has proved that intelligence is not confined to the brain cells, but that we think as a whole, that all the cell life takes part in the thinking process.

Scientists tell us that the individual cells in a piece of flesh taken from any part of the body and placed near a certain drug which is injurious to cell life will draw away as far as they can from this injurious substance. On the other hand, when a substance friendly to cell life is placed near it the cells will draw as close as possible to this friendly substance and apparently try to absorb it. In other words, these cells manifest the power of intelligent selection, or choice.

One reason why our mental attitudes, our hopes, our fears, our joys, our sorrows, have such a tremendous influence upon our bodies, our lives, is because, as Edison says, every cell in us thinks. And since this is true, we know that every thought, every impression made on the mind, every mental attitude, affects all of the cells of the body, affects the whole organism.

We have been so accustomed to confining intelligence to the brain alone that it is difficult to think it is a product of the cellular activity of the entire body, – brain, muscles, bones, tissues, and all. In fact, we think all over. The mind is the product of activity in all the cells of the body.

The latest scientific investigations seem to show that each one of the tiny microscopic cells of a body, invisible to the naked eye, contains in itself the creative, reproducing, repairing, recreating qualities, determining the entire future of the body which these cells compose; containing the plan, the development, the limitation of growth, that is, physically considered.

Each cell is endowed with intelligence and has a consciousness of its own, and, although each one of these cells has a separate consciousness, the communal, or community cells all work together for the federation of the whole in a most orderly, scientific manner. They build, repair, renew, and maintain the entire organism of the body.

Professor Nels Quevli in his latest book, "Cell Intelligence," says, "The cell is a conscious intelligent being, and by reason thereof plans and builds all plants and animals in the same manner as man constructs houses, railroads and other structures." He believes that the individual cells of any animal, acting harmoniously with the entire organism, alter the plan of the animal to meet any new demand caused by the changes of habitat of the animal, such as environment, or the changes made in response to the demand for the creature's protection, as in the case of the animals which change their colors to correspond to the coloring of the trees or the rocks upon which they live so as to make them invisible to their enemies.

Referring to the modification of the cells in the organism to meet the new demand of the animals, Professor Quevli says of the giraffe's neck, that the primitive giraffe was forced to rely less and less upon grass and more on the leaves of trees for his food. The intelligent cells of his body began (by means of the sub-division of the cells) to lift him up on his four legs, and to stretch out his neck.

To a similar necessity the cells of the elephant species threw out his snout into a long tree trunk with a pair of handy fingers at the tip.

This scientist believes that the cells in any part of the body contain a property of memory reaching back through the ages to the primordial cells, to the beginning of life itself, and that this, with other characteristics have been passed along by the divisions of the cells. These qualities are preserved when the cells divide. All the qualities which were in the original cell before the division are passed along to each of the new halves. The new cells formed are really a part of the old one; contain everything which the original cell contained.

The cells do not increase in size with the growth of the animal which they build. The growth comes from the division of the cells, thus multiplying them. This process keeps up, for example, in the infant, until it has attained its full growth, that is, until it has filled out the plan in the individual cells themselves.

"You can clearly see," says the professor, "the skill and experience possessed by the cells, or, more correctly speaking, by the individuals composing the cells, and which they have accumulated through the vast ages of experience and handed on to posterity and preserved."

We are apt to think of the body as a collection of different organs and that these organs are in a way separate, of different material or construction. But we are simply one enormous mass of tiny cells closely related to one another. Because the bones, for example, are harder than the brain, we think there can be little affinity between them, but, as a matter of fact, all the twelve different tissues of the body are made up of cells of varying consistency, all of which have come from one primordial cell – and what affects one cell anywhere in the body affects all. Each cell is an entity or little self, and we are made up of these billions of our little selves or cells.

These tiny selves are like members of a great orchestra which instantly respond to the keynote given them by their leader. Whatever tune our mentality plays, they play. They become like our thought. Every suggestion, every motive that moves the individual, is reflected in these cells. Every cell in the body vibrates in unison with every thought, every emotion, every passion that sways us, and the result on the cell life corresponds with the character of the thought, the emotion or passion.

The ego is the master spirit, the leader of all the little self or cell communities. All the cells of the body will do its bidding. The ego can think health into the cells or it can think disease. It can think discord or harmony into them. It can think efficiency or inefficiency into them. It can send a success thrill or a failure thrill through all of the cells, a thrill of masterfulness or of weakness. It can send through them a vibration of fear or of courage, of selfishness or of generosity. It can send vibrating through all the cells of the body a thrill of hope or of despair, a thrill of love or of hate; a triumphant vibration or a vibration of defeat, of failure, of disgrace. In short, whatever thought the ego, or I, sends out will stamp itself on every cell in the body, will make it like itself.

Surgeons report that after a great victory, for instance, the wounds of the soldiers, as has been noticed in many similar instances, heal much more rapidly than the wounds of the soldiers in the defeated army, showing that the mental exhilaration, which accompanies the consciousness of victory, is a stimulant, a tonic, while conversely the despondency, which accompanies defeat, is also a physical depressant.

The cells are practically an extension of the brain. Each is a substation connected with the central station of the brain. Anger, hatred, jealousy or malice in the brain means anger, hatred, jealousy or malice in every cell in the body. Trouble in the brain means trouble everywhere. Happiness in the brain means happiness everywhere. When the mind is full of hope, bright prospects, the body is full of hope, alert, efficient, eager to work. When there is discouragement in the mind there is discouragement, despondency everywhere in the body. Ambition is paralyzed, enthusiasm blighted, efficiency strangled.

For a long time surgeons have known that certain kinds of cancer are produced by mental influences; that not only cancerous tendencies latent in the system are thus aroused and their development encouraged, but that some kinds of cancers, even when there is no previous hereditary tendency or taint may be absolutely originated in this way. This scientific conclusion has been tremendously emphasized by the great increase in the development of cancer in those who have been hard hit by the war, especially those who have lost relatives or dear friends, or whose loved ones have been frightfully mangled, maimed for life. Their peculiar mental suffering, the mingled worry, grief and anxiety of these people has aggravated cancerous tendencies and originated many new cases of cancer where no previous tendencies to that dread disease existed.

A great Paris specialist, Dr. Theodore Truffler, cites a case where a patient who showed no predisposition whatever to cancer developed it after much mourning for the loss of his two sons in battle. This grief had simulated into a real cancer eruption which before had been apparently unimportant.

Not only do worry, fear, and anxiety and great grief induce cancer, but hatred, grudges, chronic jealousy, also originate several different kinds of cancer, and very materially hasten the development of cancerous tendencies which they do not originate.

Many kinds of skin disease, kidney trouble, dyspepsia, liver trouble, brain and heart trouble, are now known to result from mental causes, such as chronic hatred and jealousy. These keep the blood and other secretions in a state of chronic poisoning, which devitalizes the whole body and encourages the development of latent disease tendencies or of disease germs.

Every physician knows that discouragement is a depressant, that melancholia will greatly increase the activity and hasten the development of physical diseases. We little realize what we are doing when we are constantly sending messages of discouragement, of fear, of worry through all the billions of cells in the body. We little realize what it means when we talk discouragement, when we give up to the "blues," when we lose courage, faith, hope, and confidence in ourselves. It really means panic, disorganization, all through the cell life of the body. Mental depression is felt in every remotest cell. It unnerves every organ, and reduces the entire organism to a state of weakness and inefficiency, if not to utter collapse.

This is the reason why people sometimes fall in a faint from the shock of bad news, when sudden death or a frightful accident comes to those dear to them. The painful sensation it causes is not all in the head; it is not all in the brain. The effect of the shock visits every cell in the body. They are depressed all over. The whole cell life feels the shock. Every bit of bad, discouraging news, depression, fear, worry, anxiety, jealousy, hatred, – these send their disintegrating messages through all the cell colonies, all the dependencies in the body.

On the other hand, good news, the expectation of better things, the renewal of hope, confidence, the up-building of faith in glorious things that are coming in the near future – these act like a tonic on those who are "down and out." They refresh and renew the entire being.

The trouble is we have been so in the habit of thinking of the body outside of the brain itself as a sort of unintelligent matter, absolutely dependent upon the control of the brain, that it is very difficult for us to grasp the truth that the intelligence, the planner, the builder, the repairer, is in each cell.

When we are wounded, for instance, we do not deliberately with our brain send a message to the cells to repair and rebuild where the damage has been done, where the tissues have been lacerated or cut away. The cells themselves do that, they are the builders. They built the body originally; and they maintain and repair it.

Professor Quevli says that in each division of the cell, or nucleus, a crowd of skilled workers, intelligent builders, exist. He believes in the interesting theory that the planner of the cell, the planner of the individual, is in the microscopic cell itself. How could we imagine a force molding, fashioning, creating, modifying, changing, nourishing, to exist outside of the cell life! The only sound theory is that this force or intelligence is an indestructible part of the cell life itself, that it is the great cosmic intelligence everywhere present. It is life itself; we cannot image it absent from any atom, molecule, or electron in existence, any more than we can image a spot where the mathematical law does not apply, or that two and two do not make four.

Some of our most advanced scientists believe that the cells of the different organs of the body constitute what we may term a community, mind or brain, which presides over the life and functions of each particular organ. These community brains, such as the stomach, the liver, the kidneys, the heart, get their instructions from the great central station of intelligence, – the brain.

Every cell in the body is an energetic little worker, incessantly laboring for the community to which it belongs. Take, for example, the group of cells which form the liver. The office of this organ is to secrete bile, manufacture sugar, and eliminate poisons which might be fatal to other organs, such as the kidneys. Every cell is occupied in this important work.

Another group of these tiny cell workers, that which forms the heart, are continually busy in the service of this great central organ. Its duty is to keep the blood in circulation, never to let it stop an instant, day or night.

A third group of these wonder workers form the stomach. The office of the stomach is to begin the process of digestion, to manufacture from the blood the acid which helps to disintegrate the food. It also does much of the work which the teeth were intended to do, but which we usually neglect.

Another community of cells constitutes the kidneys. Their office is to strain out of the blood the poisons which the other organs have not eliminated, and which if allowed to remain would injure the more vital organs.

Here is a group which forms the thyroid gland, whose work is to store up certain salts and other substances for future use, and to assist in regulating the nutrition and the heat of the body.

And here is another group, perhaps the most important, which forms the leader of all the other community centers – the brain. This thinking organ is the seat of distribution of all orders through the marvelous system of nerves, which run from the great central station to every corner of the body, communicating instantly with every one of the billions of the cell citizens in the whole system.

Like those in all the other organs, each cell of the brain is constantly at work. Now, these billions of workers, all specialists in their line, no cell doing the work delegated to another, are dependent on the nourishment which they get from the blood. If the blood is poor, thin, deteriorated by imperfect or insufficient food, or if it is poisoned by dissipation or by wrong thinking, then their work as builders suffers accordingly.

When the blood for any reason is thus impoverished the cells of the stomach and other digestive organs are too feeble to do their work properly. And when the food is not properly digested, it putrefies and the poisons it generates are absorbed by the body, causing trouble everywhere throughout the system. The heart action is impaired. The circulation of the blood is poor, and all the tissues suffer from lack of nutrition. The vigor of the body is depreciated, because the digestive organs cannot manufacture force, robustness, out of vitiated blood. The billions of cells suffer from malnutrition, or semi-starvation, and your powers begin to wane. There is a lack of vim and force and fire in your efforts. The cry for food, for nutrition, from the suffering cells goes to the brain. It convinces you that something is the matter, and you say you are sick, you are down and out, you don't feel like anything. Your ambition sags, and off you go to a drug store or a doctor for a tonic, a stimulant, something which will brace you up, make you feel better. Perhaps you go to a saloon and get one bracer after another, with nothing but feeble, temporary results. Then you begin to fear you are going to be laid up, that you are developing some disease. The terrors of a possible breakdown add its poisoned burden to the already poor, vitiated blood, and matters grow worse.

Instead of radically remedying such an unfortunate condition by satisfying the intelligent cry of the cells, most people begin to add the whip to the tired horse as a stimulant, a tonic, when the horse needs nothing but good wholesome food and rest, harmony in the mental kingdom.

Everywhere in the body Nature tries to save us from our ignorance, our mistakes, our animal appetites, our dissipations, our wrong thinking. Every cell in the body is constantly on guard, trying to help us, trying to save us from our own ignorance and sins.

Much of what we call intuitive perception is due to the cell intelligence in the various parts of the body. What is it, for instance, that tells us when we have eaten enough to supply the bodily needs? The brain does not know it, because none of the food which we eat at an ordinary meal has had time to affect the brain before the appetite has been satisfied. What is the appetite? It is the demand for nourishment from the different cells of the body. It is not located in any one place. The cells call for food, and it is their intelligence that makes this call. We say we instinctively feel when we have eaten enough. We do not want any more and our appetite declines. But this knowledge does not come from the brain alone. It is a feeling of all the cells of the body, that there is sufficient in the stomach to supply its needs. The appetite wanes accordingly, but it must be intelligence back of this which makes this decision. The brain cells simply make a call for their own needs; they do not make calls for the liver, the heart, the kidneys, the muscles.

The mental healing of disease rests upon the fact that intelligence is not confined to the brain, but that there is intelligence in the cells of the body generally, as has been proved in the case of the deaf, dumb and blind. In their efforts at self-expression these people have developed the intelligence of the finger tips to such an extent that actual gray matter cells, similar to those in the brain, have been found there. In other words, gray brain cells are developed in the fingertips of the blind.

It is well known that this gray brain matter found in the fingertips of the blind is also found in other parts of the system, especially in many ramifications of the spinal nerves. It is found everywhere along the tract of the nervous system.

Walking and all of the involuntary movements of the body are controlled by the intelligence of the local cells. We do not stop and premeditate, or will, every step. We take each one automatically, without any exercise of the will. An intelligence outside the brain must also keep up the heart beats and the breathing while the brain is unconscious during sleep, and even while we are awake, for we make no conscious effort at any time to keep up these functions.

Nor does the expert pianist think of the movements of his fingers when he is playing. In fact, he may all the time be thinking of something else. His mind may be wandering, and yet he plays intelligently because intelligent cells are distributed throughout his muscular nervous system.

To say that the brain educates the spinal column and the nervous branches to perform this piano miracle is no scientific explanation. The only satisfactory explanation is that all the cells of the body are intelligent, that we think as a whole. We have inherited the race belief that thinking is confined to the brain. But the fact is the difference between the brain cells and the cells in other parts of the body is not nearly so great as we once thought. Many brain accidents have shown that the destruction of large portions of the brain tissue does not materially affect the power of thought, any more than the destruction of tissue in other parts of the body affects it. Not only this, but large portions of the brain have been removed, and yet the individual has gone on with his work apparently as before. Here is an interesting experiment performed by a noted scientist which gives a striking proof of cell intelligence outside of the brain. This experiment has been tried again and again.

"If a drop of acid is placed on the lower surface of the thigh of a frog after its head has been cut off, the decapitated frog will rub off the drop of acid with the upper surface of the foot on the same leg. Scientists have cut off this foot after the head was cut off, and the headless animal, after trying time and again to rub off the acid with the same foot as before, will finally use the foot on the other leg and continue until it succeeds in rubbing off the acid."

Here we certainly have proof of intelligence combined with harmonious contractions in order to bring about certain definite results. It is a proof that an intelligent mind acts without a brain.

We know that the brain carries on but a small part of the work of the bodily organism. All of our involuntary movements, the manufacture of the fluids of the body, of the bodily secretions, the changing of foods into tissues, are not affected by the voluntary brain. The work of the chemical laboratory in the body, which is simply beyond human comprehension, is all carried on by intelligent organ cells outside of the brain. The brain cells, it is true, are more highly sensitized, more responsive, than the cells of some other parts of the body. They form, so to speak, a sort of mouthpiece for the other cells, and this is where they find their outward expression.

There is no doubt that the billions of cells composing the body all belong to one intelligent whole. What affects one cell affects all, so that whatever passes through the brain cells passes through every other cell in the body. We know how instantaneously news, a sudden shock of any sort, received at the central brain station is sent to all the organs. The heart, the kidneys, the liver, all of them are at once affected by it. This shows how intimately they must be tied together. The entire body is evidently a sort of an extended brain.

If someone should scratch one end of a piece of timber a hundred feet long with a nail, and your ear were at the other end of the timber, you could hear the scratch instantly. The distance does not seem to make any difference in the transmission of the sound. In a similar way, every thought, every mood, every emotion goes instantly to every part of the body. For example, you may have just sat down to your Thanksgiving dinner with a ravenous appetite, when the gastric juice is trickling from every gastric follicle in your stomach, and you suddenly receive a telegram announcing a terrible catastrophe, in which some of those dearest to you have been mutilated or killed. Instantly the gastric follicles cease to generate the gastric juice and become dry and parched, as does the tongue in a fever. The heart and the other organs feel the shock at the same time and are equally distressed, and their action inhibited. In short, the different organs and functions respond instantly to the painful news, showing that whatever enters the mind goes immediately to the entire cell life of the body.

The condition of your cells, of your tissues, of your organs, will depend upon the message which you send to them through your thought, through your convictions regarding them, whether of strength or weakness, of health or disease. You think clear through every cell to the farthest extremities of your body. And as you think regarding your cells so they are. Their fate is largely in your hands. They will obey whatever orders you give them. By your mental attitude toward the cells of the various organ communities you can make your physical organs perform their functions normally or abnormally; you can insure health or bring about disease; you can prolong your life or you can shorten it.

We know that by concentrating our thought intensely upon any part

of the body the blood vessels in that organ or locality expand, and an extra supply of blood is sent there. In other words, the blood follows the thought. Professor Alexander Graham Bell told me that when on long riding trips in Halifax, in severe weather, he could warm his feet by concentrating his thought upon them, so that in a short time they would be all aglow. This method of quickening the circulation of the blood has been tried so often that scientists no longer question it.

Elmer Gates has often tried the following experiment as a proof of the power of mind in this direction. Immersing his hands in two separate vessels of water just even full, he would first concentrate his thought on the right hand until the water in the vessel would overflow; then reversing, he would concentrate on the left until that vessel would overflow.

These experiments give a little idea of what thought can do in stimulating or depressing the blood, on which the life of the body depends – "for the blood is the life."

It is well known that the fear thought, the thought, for example, that you have Bright's disease, or that you have inherited, and are developing, tuberculosis, causes congestion in that part of your anatomy on which it is fixed. And if the fear thought becomes chronic you will have chronic congestion there, which will aid in developing the thing you fear.

Take the case of a young girl who is told by her friends that she has probably inherited tuberculosis, because one or both of her parents died of that disease. If every time she is exposed to inclement weather, gets her feet wet, or gets in a draft, she is reminded that she is taking great chances, she develops a fear thought. She concentrates this fear upon her lungs, causing congestion there, irritation, coughing. This increases her fear and causes loss of appetite.

Then, of course, she loses nourishment, and there is a general decline in her physical condition. Naturally a loss in weight follows. This symptom frightens her still more, because victims of tuberculosis are always weighing themselves, imagining they are shrinking. Her fears cause imperfect digestion, imperfect assimilation, and hence imperfect repair and renewal of lost tissue. She begins to lose color and then everybody tells her that she is not looking well. This loss of color is another dread symptom, and so it goes on until the fear, the conviction that she is developing the fateful disease, cuts down the last remnant of her disease-resisting power, and she falls a victim to any latent tubercular germs in her system. She stamps her fear thought on the cell life of her lungs and other organs until they respond to it, become like it. Multitudes of people have tubercular germs in their system which never develop if they hold the health thought and build up a strong disease-resisting power.

Disease germs feed upon the debris or broken-down tissue in the body. They are scavengers and do not feed upon healthy tissue, healthy food. But when the tissues begin to break down through fear, the disease-resisting power deteriorates rapidly, until the body gets below what we may call the health line. Then all sorts of scavengers or enemy germs, waiting for their opportunity, begin to feed upon the broken-down tissue; the blood becomes impoverished, and the disease gets a hold on its victim.

There is no doubt that disease in the various organs is often due to utter discouragement which the organ cells have received from the central station – the brain. The cells of the whole body often give up their struggle for life because of the discouragement of the master cells. Time and again when the heart had ceased to beat, and apparently the last breath had been taken, life has been called back to a seemingly dead body just by strong reassuring words, by arousing and restoring the lost confidence of the cells. When there is supreme confidence of victory in all of the cells of the body, life will not depart. But when the cells in the different organ communities get from the brain the message that the death sentence has been pronounced by the physician, or when the patient gives this fatal prognosis as his own conviction, then there is no hope for the dependent communities to try to save the situation.

Is it strange that the cells of the diseased organs should give up the struggle and cease to fight for life when the brain has given up hope and sent a message of despair through the whole system? These impaired cells were having a hard time of it before. There was probably a panic in the little cell community, and now, when the grand commander of all of the cells of the body gives up, the depending organ communities also naturally give up.

On the other hand, when the cells all through the body get the thrill of confidence, of hope, of faith in their strength, from the center of intelligence, then they are comparatively free from danger of death. There is enough vitality, enough latent energy in many a body which has just breathed its last to re-energize and bring it back to life again if such confidence could be restored to the mind that it would utilize the latent force in the apparently dead cells.

Since thought has such a tremendous influence upon the cell life of the body, how important it is that our thoughts and images and emotions should be friendly and not hostile, should be helpful and not injurious! How imperative that we hold only those images in the mind, visualize only those things which are beneficial, kindly, uplifting to the body, not those things which tend to devitalize, to dwarf and ruin it!

The essential thing is to keep the cells in all of the organs happy, contented, encouraged, and harmonious. If we do this, we shall be happy, contented, and harmonious ourselves. That is, the resultant of the harmonious action of the entire cell life of the body must be efficiency, harmony and happiness for the whole man.

Every time you allow a vicious thought, a despondent thought, a thought of failure, of fear, of poverty to enter your mind, every time you allow a foreboding of some threatening event to take hold of you, every time you indulge in jealousy, in envy, in hatred, in revenge, in any evil emotion, every cell in your body is correspondingly affected. So, too, they take on your enthusiasm, your zest, your cheer, your courage, your faith. They are encouraged or discouraged; they expand or contract their possibilities at your suggestion.

What you think about the cells of any organ they will return to you in kind. You can no more get the best from the cells of your stomach, and your other digestive organs, for instance, when you are all the time saying uncomplimentary things about them, always discouraging them, abusing them, than you can get the best out of your employees or your children by the same methods. When you treat them in this way, talk against them, antagonize them, they become depressed, and express resentment in nonperformance of their functions.

If we treated our children or our employees as many of us treat the millions of tiny cells in our stomach, our liver, our kidneys, or other organs; if we were constantly complaining of them, condemning them for not doing their work better, if we were suspicious of them, watching them and always fearing they would play us false, we certainly would not get the best out of them.

Imagine what a pessimistic, dyspeptic grumbler will do to the cells during a life time of fault-finding, of discouraging suggestions! Think what a man does to his digestive organs who is always saying they are no good, that they have gone back on him, that they cannot digest anything which he likes, and that he can only eat the things which he despises! Is it any wonder that he has chronic dyspepsia when he swallows a mouthful of dyspepsia with every mouthful of food, and then continually hammers away and denounces his digestive organs between meals? Think of what this mental attitude means not only to his digestive organs but to the other organs of his body!

If you suffer from indigestion, it is because you don't believe that your digestive organs can take proper care of your food. You suffer because you expect to suffer. You get what you expect. There is everything in expecting your body to perform all its functions normally, healthfully. Think of your human machine as perfect; treat your organs as though they were normal. Expect your body, all the cell communities, to express harmony, not discord. Don't harbor a suspicious attitude toward any of your physical organs. Believe that they are going to do the work which they were intended to do, and to do it properly. Trust them just as you would trust your children, your employees. Believe in them, and treat them kindly. Instead of blaming and abusing, encourage and praise them, and they will perform their functions normally and give you robust health.

If the cells in any organ are diseased, the health suggestion, the health affirmation, the holding of the health ideal in the brain will tend to heal them. To send life currents of healing thought sweeping through any defective or diseased organ tends to stimulate the cell life, to encourage the cell organization, – the stomach, the kidneys, the heart, the liver, the lungs, etc. – to respond to the optimistic suggestion. In other words, thinking health, thinking life and truth into a diseased organ, tends to destroy the disease infection, to arouse latent life force in the cells, and to bring about normal health conditions.

We know that we get out of the various organs about what we expect. The brain is no exception. Expect nothing, get nothing. If you have no confidence in your brain it will return only weakness or mediocrity to you. On the other hand, if you have a firm, vigorous faith in it, if you expect great things from it, it will match your expectation.

The same is true of the muscles of every part of the body. Believe in your muscles, trust them, believe they are strong and vigorous, have faith that you can lift an enormous weight or can perform great feats as an athlete, and your five hundred muscles will come to your rescue and redeem your faith.

This is true even of animals. When the race horse has lost confidence in its speed it never regains it. As long as the animal believes he can beat the others in the race he wins. But when it has been beaten a few times it gets the habit of being beaten, and cannot regain its confidence. It believes it is going to be beaten, and it is.

The art of radiating health thoughts through and through the whole system until every nerve and fiber, every cell in the body, feels the electric thrill of the health force, is the art of arts. It means the achievement of perfect health, of perfect efficiency and of perfect happiness.

Just as we can antidote disease in the cell life by health thoughts, in a similar way we can send out from the central brain station thoughts of prosperity, of opulence, thoughts of success, affirmations of power, that will antidote the poverty disease.

By constantly affirming your divinity, the truth of your being, the reality of you, as one with God, holding the thought that God is your health, that He is in every atom, in every electron, that He is in every cell in your body, and that His presence excludes all sickness, disease and weakness, all lack and unhappiness, you will impress the consciousness of God's presence on every cell of your being, and then you cannot be anything but well, happy and prosperous.

No colds, no rheumatism, no cancerous poisons, no tubercular germs, no fear, no unhappiness, no discord of any kind, can exist in you when you are vitally conscious of God's presence in every cell in your body. While you feel conscious of your oneness with the One, that every cell in you is one with Him, because all life is the one life, the expression of the one vitality which pervades the universe, you cannot suffer in any part of your being.

The consciousness of God, the consciousness that He fills every cell in our body, that there can be no discord, no disease, no weakness where God is; that where God is, all is health, all is beauty, that God is truth and the truth makes you free, because it is the truth of your being, – this consciousness of your oneness with God makes you free from the enemies of your health, your success and your happiness.

Stamp this God-consciousness on every cell in your body. Cling to this one thought of God's allness and everywhereness, that there can be nothing but God, that wherever you look, wherever you go, all is God, and that because there is nothing but God, all is good and there is nothing but good, everything which does not seem to be good, having no reality, being but the absence of good. Hold this thought constantly, and you will be free from all the enemies of your being.

If we would triumph over all our limitations, we must impress the triumphant thought on every cell. We must radiate through the body not only thoughts of health and strength, but also of courage, hope, confidence, expectation of better conditions. Instead of radiating through our system, as most of us do, the poverty thought, the lack thought, the conviction that we are the slaves of social and economic systems above which we cannot rise, we must radiate the abundance thought, the freedom thought, the expectation of prosperity, of opulence. Instead of stamping the failure thought, the thought of mediocrity, or incompetence upon our cells, we must stamp upon them the conviction of superb ability, of confidence that we can accomplish what we undertake, because we are in partnership with God, and in close touch with divine supply. We must constantly cultivate the habit of radiating the thought triumphant, the habit of radiating masterfulness instead of weakness.

After a little practice in the cultivation of up-building thought, the health thought, the success thought, the happy thought, the vibrations will reach every remotest cell in our bodies, and we shall feel the thrill of health, of hopefulness, of expectancy of better things animating and energizing our whole being.

What we think and believe we create. Hence, if we would always hold the ideal suggestion of everything in life, the ideal suggestion of health, the ideal suggestion of our ability, of our efficiency, the ideal suggestion regarding our career, our success, our happiness, the ideal suggestion of our destiny, it would transform our lives, it would lift us from the common to the uncommon. It would make us artists in life instead of mere artisans.

10
HEART-TO-HEART TALKS WITH YOURSELF

> **THE POSITIVE man keys his life to the "I can" note; the negative man to the "I can't."**
>
> **Say to yourself "Health, luck, usefulness, success are mine, I claim them."**
>
> **Keep thinking that thought, no matter what happens. —Ella Wheeler Wilcox.**

"My words are spirit and they are truth; and they shall not return to me void; but shall accomplish that whereunto they were sent." How many of us grasp the real significance of this Biblical utterance? Or of this other: "And the word was made flesh and dwelt among us"? How many of us ever think that our own words, our uttered thoughts are living forces and are made flesh? Yet it is literally true that they are being out pictured in our body, are chiseling our physique, shaping our faces, molding our expression to their likeness. What we think and say reappears not only in our expression, but also in our physical condition, in our health, good or bad, according to the nature of our thoughts and words. Every word we speak is an indestructible force, because it affirms a thought, a sentiment, an emotion, a motive, which never ceases to exert its power.

Jesus evidently recognized that words are real forces, for He said, "Heaven and earth shall pass away, but my word shall not pass away."

Material things might pass away, but His word was a force which could never cease to exercise its power. All through the Bible the power of the word is emphasized. "The Word was made flesh and dwelt among us," "The Word was with God, and the Word was God," "He sent His Word and healed them."

There is a mysterious power in the spoken word, in the vigorous affirmation of a thought, which registers a profound impression on the subconscious mind, and the silent forces within us proceed to make the word flesh, to make the thing we affirm a reality. There is a tremendous constructive power in registering your vow, in vigorous, determined affirmation, backed by a persistent, dogged endeavor to bring about the thing we desire.

A very striking proof of this was afforded in the European war, in the awful conflict at Verdun in 1916. As stated in a telegraphed report from a high French officer, the fundamental secret of French resistance to the terrific German onslaught was psychological. It was, he said, autosuggestion on a vast scale. General Petain replaced doubt and discouragement with iron determination when throughout the entire army flashed his expressed resolution that the Germans should not get through the French lines – "Ils ne passeront pas." (They shall not pass.) All of the soldiers were so hypnotized by the constant repetition of the phrase, Ils ne passeront pas" that no idea save that of resistance could enter their heads.

There is no doubt that it trebled and quadrupled the resisting power of the army. The mighty suggestion of invincibility in the words was literally the decisive factor in the battle. The repetition of "They shall not pass," was what enabled the infantry to undergo unexampled bombardment and then rush forward with the bayonet as eagerly as fresh troops. It was the explanation of confidence in victory seen even in captured Frenchmen which amazed their German captors.

The French officer's report further stated that a surgeon in the dressing station close to the front said the most remarkable thing about the wounded was their general attitude of determination. In some cases, the faces seemed fixed with an expression of ferocious resolution, especially among those suffering from shell shocks, and the soldiers only partially conscious would repeat at intervals of their delirium, "Passeront pas, passeront pas."

All of the soldiers at Verdun were obsessed by this one dominating idea to the exclusion of everything else. "The Germans shall not pass." A correspondent at the front said: "I saw a regiment coming back to rest after six days in the trenches. The soldiers all seemed animated by a spirit of intense determination and iron resolution. When asked their opinion of the battle, the general reply was just this: 'The Germans shall not pass.' And the Germans did not pass."

Suppose you should register in your subconsciousness regarding the entrance into your mind of destructive thoughts, motives and emotions, the bitter enemies of your success and happiness, a grim resolution such as the French soldiers at Verdun registered regarding the Germans, what would happen? If whenever enemy thoughts or emotions tried to get entrance to your mental kingdom you should grimly say to them, "You shall not pass. I will not allow in my mind any enemies of my success and happiness," do you think it would be possible for them to get by? Why, of course they couldn't. It would be impossible. And if you should iterate and reiterate the same grim resolve regarding hindering habits, regarding every temptation that makes an appeal to you, "You shall not pass?" Why, my friend, this would revolutionize your life.

Every word we speak, even uttered thought, is power for good or ill, and we must remember that it is what we put into the word that gives it its meaning, and determines its quality and its force. Words themselves are the clothes for our thoughts. We can take a word and think love into it, think service into it, think friendliness into it, and it will create a corresponding feeling in the one it is addressed to. Or we can take the same word and think hatred into it, think jealousy into it, think envy into it, and hurl it out and arouse antagonism, jealousy, hatred or envy in another mind. We know that we can do the same thing with a dog, and he will feel the thought – the love or the hate, the anger or the contempt – which we put into the word. We can fling out hatred and bitterness, sarcasm, malice, in words; we can arouse the anger which kills, or we can call out love, admiration, sympathy, friendship. Everything depends upon the thought behind the word. It is the mental attitude that gives the word its real meaning. And your words are messengers of life or death to yourself and to others.

Words have put civilization where it is today. The word wedded to the thought has built everything that man has achieved. He speaks and it is done, just as God spoke and the earth was created, man and every living thing was created. Everything is made out of God's thoughts, out of God's ideas, and He speaks through man.

There is a force in spoken words which is not stirred by going over the same words mentally. When vocalized they make a more lasting impression upon the mind. You know how much more powerfully you are impressed and inspired by listening to a great lecture or sermon than you would be if you read the same thing in print. We remember the spoken word when we forget the cold type which carries thought to the brain. It makes a deeper impression on the inner self.

We can talk to our inner or other self, just as we would talk to a child; and we know from experience that it will listen to and act on our suggestions. We are constantly sending suggestions or commands to this inner self. We may not do so audibly, but we do so silently, mentally. Unconsciously we advise, we suggest, we try to influence it in certain directions.

By consciously, audibly addressing it, in heart-to-heart talks with ourselves, we find that we can very materially influence our habits, our motives, our methods of living. In fact, the possibilities of influencing the character and the life by this means are practically limitless.

Many people have killed character enemies, peace and happiness enemies, have doubled and quadrupled their self-confidence, have strengthened tremendously their initiative, their executive ability; have literally made themselves over, by heart-to-heart talks with themselves.

I know a man who has so completely changed his timid, self-effacing nature by talks with his other self that no one would dream that only a few years ago he was so shy, so extremely sensitive, that he would blush scarlet if attention were called to him in any gathering, and he would avoid people in every possible way.

Five years ago no amount of money would have induced this man to get up in a public meeting, even to put a motion or to make the simplest statement. I think he would have fainted away at the mere calling of his name in a public place. Not only had he no confidence whatever in himself, but he had a haunting obsession that he was a fraud. Although a perfectly honest, earnest, hard-working man, with good intentions toward all, he could not help feeling that in some way he was not genuine, and that sometime something would happen to show him up in his true light.

For years he suffered untold tortures from his foolish imaginings about himself. Conscious that he had ability, but cursed with weaknesses that made it in many ways unavailable, his life was headed towards failure when he accidentally came across a book which told him of the miracles possible through the practice of self-encouragement, and especially audible self-encouragement. He began immediately to carry out the suggestions of the book, and made a daily habit of heart-to-heart talks with himself. In a very short time he was conscious of a great improvement in his feelings, his mental attitude, and his spirits. Many people noticed an improvement in his manner and bearing. And now he presides at public meetings without the slightest feeling of self-consciousness. His painful shyness has vanished; he can stand any amount of criticism and denunciation without a sign of sensitiveness or embarrassment.

There is no fault, no weakness, great or small, which will not succumb to persistent, audible autosuggestion. Not only this, but it tends to arouse slumbering qualities within us which mere thinking does not stir up or waken. Most people are only half alive, half-awake to their possibilities. We all need stirring up. There is gunpowder enough in us to make a tremendous explosion if we could only get the spark to the giant powder that is sleeping within us.

If you are timid, doubting, fearful of failure, or poverty, you can reinforce your courage and strengthen your confidence in yourself by daily heart-to-heart talks with your inner self, by the frequent affirmation of the positive assertions "I must," "I can," "I will." There is no better suggestion than Emerson's for stiffening the will and the power to do: "Nerve us with incessant affirmatives." And incessant affirmatives will nerve us.

The perpetual affirmation of the power to achieve one's ambition, of one's grim determination to win out in life at any cost; the affirmation of health, of prosperity, of success, the constant assertion of confidence in one's self, of the belief in his ability to do the thing that he has set his heart on, will nerve a weak will and brace up a wavering purpose as nothing else can.

If you are not satisfied with your progress so far, if you are not growing bigger and broader in character, more efficient in your work, something is holding you back, hindering you from making your ideal real. Find out what it is and then remove it by audible self-treatments.

The best way to find what is your stumbling block is to have a frequent heart-to-heart talk with yourself. Look into your own soul and take an account of your personal stock, your success and failure qualities. Analyze yourself as you would a friend you were anxious to help, and whose strong and weak points you could see clearly.

Get by yourself in your room, or, infinitely better, in some quiet place in the country where you can be absolutely alone with your Maker, and examine yourself something after this fashion, putting the questions aloud, and addressing yourself by name:

"Now (James or Ann, or whatever your name is) what is the trouble with you? Why do you not get along faster? Do you lack ambition or has it not yet been awakened? Why are you not doing at least as well as others around you are doing under similar conditions? Why are you plodding along in mediocrity while those all about you with no better chances, perhaps infinitely poorer chances than yours, are getting on by leaps and bounds? There must be some reason for this? Do you lack vitality, energy; or are you not using what you have? Have you some weakness, defect or peculiarity which is holding you down? Are you the victim of a weak link in the chain of your character which is nullifying all your efforts in other directions? Where is the trouble? You must put your finger on it and correct it or your life may be a failure."

Write out a list of the qualities that make a strong, courageous, successful character, and their opposites, those that make a weak, timid, unsuccessful one, and examine yourself to see what your rating in the list is. Call them off aloud – faith, courage, self-confidence, ambition, enthusiasm, perseverance, concentration, initiative, cheerfulness, optimism, thoroughness, etc. Ask yourself if you possess these splendid qualities, or if you incline to their opposites.

Don't be afraid to face your weak points, or your fool streaks, to call your faults by their right names. Bring them into the light, see them for what they are, and then grapple with them. You cannot afford to be less than God intended you to be, to be less than you feel that you should be and can be, to have your life spoiled by some defect which you can overcome.

When you have gone over the specific character qualities ask yourself these broader questions; always visualizing and addressing yourself by name: "What are you here for? What do you mean to the world? What message does your life, your career, bring to it? What do you mean to your community? What do you stand for? What do you represent? Do you realize that you were sent here with a message for humanity? Are you delivering it like a man, like a woman, patiently, persistently, determinedly, without grumbling, whining or shirking? What are you giving to the world? Do you mean much of anything to anybody but yourself? Is your sole aim self-aggrandizement, to get more reputation, more money, more comforts for yourself? Does your ambition as far as possible shut others out of your life? Are you always going to do the kindly deed, going to help others in the future, when you get on a little further, when you are better able, when all your own wants are satisfied? Are you dreaming of the big thing you are going to do tomorrow, or are you doing the little things which you can do today, giving yourself as you go along; giving, if you have nothing else to give, encouragement, inspiration, helpfulness to those on the way with you? Would your community miss you very much if you should drop out of it?"

Probe yourself in this manner until you get a good line on yourself, a fair estimate of yourself; until you know both your strength and your weakness; until you can see with clear eyes the things that are keeping you back, the lack in your nature that is handicapping you, the weakness that is cutting down the average of your ability by ten, twenty, fifty or even seventy-five per cent. Then vigorously attack your enemies, – the enemies of your success, of your efficiency, of your happiness. Constantly stoutly affirm your complete mastery over them, their powerlessness to dominate your life and ruin your career.

If, for instance, you are a victim of self-effacement; if you find you lack self-confidence, if you never dare undertake any responsibility you can possibly avoid, if, instead of asserting your individuality and assuming the dignity that is yours by divine right, you shrink from everything which draws attention to yourself; if you have no faith in your ability, you must talk to yourself something like this:

"I am a child of God. I am made in His image and likeness. I am a partaker of all His divine qualities. Therefore I have divine power; I have strength and ability to do what I long to do. I am strength. I am ability. I am self-confidence. I am success. I can do what I will to do, and will no longer suffer this cowardly timidity to rule me. I will never again by self-depreciation and self-effacement, deny my divine Fatherhood. It is a sin against my Father and myself to belittle my heritage from Him. I am the son of an all-powerful King, and henceforth I will act the part. I will walk the earth like a prince. I will never again shrink from assuming any responsibility which comes to me. I have plenty of ability to do what I long to do, to be what I long to be. I will no longer go about as if I were inferior to others. I am not inferior, and from now on I shall express my opinion and assert myself whenever and wherever necessary.

"I am now facing life with a self-respecting, confident attitude, with a hopeful outlook, for I know that as a child of God I am victory-organized. Self-depreciation is a crime, a reflection upon my Creator who pronounced everything He made good. Lack of faith in myself is nothing but lack of faith in Him. I will cut it out of my life, for I am that which I think I am. I can be nothing more, nothing less. As a child of Omnipotence, of the All-Good, I am bound to make good in every detail of my life. I owe this to my Father and to myself."

By heart-to-heart talks of this sort with yourself you can change your whole nature, revolutionize your career. Whether it is faith, courage, initiative, cheerfulness, whatever it is you lack, assume the quality you wish to possess, affirm positively that it is already yours, exercise it whenever possible, concentrate on it, and you will be surprised how quickly you can acquire the desired. I am a great believer in the building power of affirmation; in the possibilities in persistently affirming the thing I am determined to do, in strengthening qualities in which I am weak, in building character, in making life noble.

The following strong, positive affirmations by C. D. Larson are very suggestive and would make a splendid daily exercise:

- *I will become more than I am.*

- *I will achieve more because I know that I can.*
- *I will recognize only that which is good in myself; that which is good in others.*
- *I will be more determined when adversity threatens than ever in my life to prove that I can turn all things to good account.*
- *I will wish only for that which can give freedom and truth, which can add to the welfare of the race.*
- *I will always speak to give encouragement, inspiration and joy.*
- *I will work to be of service to an ever increasing number; and my ruling desire shall be to enrich, ennoble and beautify existence for all who may come my way.*

When you assert yourself, assert the spiritual "I," the God image in you, not the physical "I," the flesh of you. This would be mere egotism, and it is not asserting your egotism that will benefit you. This will only hurt you. But asserting the reality, the divinity of yourself will do everything for you. Your divine or real self is your potential self, your creative self, and when you assert the reality of your being, not the outward or bodily personality, you are simply asserting divinity, you are asserting omnipotence, omniscience, and you are asserting a power that can do things.

If we could only realize the creative power of affirmation, of assuming that we are the real embodiment of the thing we long to be or to attain, not that we possess all the qualities of good, but that we are these qualities, – with the constant affirming, "I myself am a part of the great creative, sustaining principle of the universe, because my real, divine self and my Father are one"—what happiness it would bring to earth's children!

Affirmation is a living, vital force. The Bible owes much of its strength to this force. It is a book of affirmations, of strong, positive statements. But for this fact it would long ago have lost its power.

There is no parleying, no arguing, no attempt by the sacred writers to prove the truth of what they say. They merely assert, affirm dogmatically that certain things happened, and that certain other things would happen. Had they attempted to prove the authenticity of what they wrote, endeavored to convince the reader that they were honest men making genuine statements, they would have aroused doubts. But there is no appeal to sympathy, no appeal to the readers' credulity, no appeal for confirmation, no posing for effect, only unrelenting positiveness, persistent affirmations. They simply state facts and affirm principles. Every line breathes dominance, superiority and confidence. In this lies their tremendous power. There is no sentimental imploring even in the Lord's Prayer. It demands. It is "give us," "lead us not," forgive us," etc.

In your talks with yourself, be like the Biblical writers. Don't wobble, or "think," or "hope." Say stoutly, "I am," "I can," "I will," "It is." Constantly, everlastingly affirm that you will become what your ambitions indicate as fitting and possible. Do not say, "I shall be a success sometime;" say "I am a success now. Success is my birthright." Do not say that you are going to be happy in the future, say to yourself, "I was intended for happiness, made for it, and I am happy now." Say with Walt Whitman, "'I, myself, am good fortune.'" Assert your actual possession of the things you need; of the qualities you long to have. Force your mind toward your goal; hold it there steadily, persistently, for this is the mental state that creates. This is what causes the word to be made flesh. The negative mind, which doubts, wavers, fears, creates nothing. It cannot send forth a positive, confident assertion.

We are constantly letting loose mighty thought forces, emotion forces, word forces which are forever multiplying and expressing themselves in the universal energy, which are forever fashioning our conditions. We are rich or poor, healthy or unhealthy, successful or unsuccessful, happy or unhappy, noble or ignoble, according to our use of our thought and word forces. The outer registration in the flesh, in all material circumstances and things, corresponds with the inner thought and the decisive positive word.

Let the spirit of you, the real self, constantly affirm the "I am," and the power you have through the All-Power. Make your affirmations quietly, but with great confidence and positiveness. Say "I am united with Him. I am able to do what He wills me to do. It is my duty to obey the inner urge of my being, that divine ambition to measure up to my highest possibilities, which ever bids me up and on. I will never again allow anything to interfere with the free and full exercise of my physical, mental and spiritual faculties. I will unfold all the possibilities that the Creator has in-folded in the ego, the I of me. There is no lost day in God's calendar, no allowance for waste, and henceforth I will make the most of the stuff that has been given me. I will play the part of a son of Omnipotence."

But remember it is the life, the driving power of the spirit that gives the word its power. If you don't mean what you say, if you don't live the meaning into your words, they are mere idle breath.

The same word, for instance, means a very different thing when spoken by people of different types of character. The same words spoken by one person will heal diseases, while spoken by another they will have no influence whatever upon the patient. The difference in results is due to the difference in the life, in the character, of the speakers. Some healers are unsuccessful, even when they are letter perfect in the intellectual understanding of the healing principle, simply because they lack the spiritual side, simply because their life does not match their teachings.

In fact, it is the life, the spiritual life that does the healing through the words which the intellect suggests. Just as faith without good works is of no avail without the spirit, without the life behind them, words are cold and ineffectual.

When you long for anything that it is right for you to have, affirm in perfect confidence that the thing is already yours; claim it as a reality; do what you can on the material plane to make it yours, and soon you will reap what you have sown in thought and in positive creative affirmation.

Say to yourself, "God is no respecter of persons. Our Father is not and could not be, partial in His treatment of His children. To all, without distinction, He gives the same love, the same rights and privileges. He will give me, through my own effort, what I need, what I ask for. I can and I will do what I long to do. I will be what I desire to be."

Make these affirmations again and again, and do not wait for an opportunity to begin the thing you want to do. Make your opportunity. The power of affirmation will work miracles for you.

You will find that, just in proportion as you increase your confidence in yourself by the affirmation of what you are determined to be and to do, your ability will increase. No matter what other people may think or say about you, never allow yourself to doubt that you can do what you will to do. Boldly, confidently assert that there is a special place for you in the world, an individual role which only you can fill, and that you are going to fill it like a man. Train yourself to expect great things of yourself. Never admit, even by your manner, that you think you are destined to do little things all your life.

The way to get the best out of yourself, to make the most of your life, is to put things right up to yourself, to handle yourself without gloves, and talk to yourself as you would talk to a very dear younger brother or sister, or to a son or daughter of whom you expect great things and whose welfare is as dear to you as your own, one whom you long to help to get on and up in the world. You can do this with marvelous results in correcting bad habits or overcoming temptations or dangerous tendencies.

In telling how he resisted the temptation to drink when "the boys" wanted him "to take a drink," Edison said: "I thought I had better use for my brain. I wanted all the brain power I could get. I wanted to increase the efficiency of my life, and not diminish it, not demoralize and benumb it. I did not want to take into my mouth an enemy to steal away my brain. I wanted to do the things which would increase, not diminish, my brain power, which would increase, not lessen, my possibilities, which would increase and not destroy, my resources; something which would increase my powers of investigation, of discovery; something which would increase my inventive ability, not destroy it, and I said to myself: 'I will let that greatest enemy of the race, that enemy which has taken hold of more men and women, ruined more careers, destroyed more happiness, than anything else in the world, alone.'"

If you are in danger of becoming a victim of drink, or if it has already laid its grip on you, say to yourself what Edison said: "I will let that greatest enemy of the race, that enemy which has taken hold of more men and women, ruined more careers, destroyed more happiness, than anything else in the world, alone. I cannot afford to give up even a small per cent of my ability to whiskey. About the only success assets I have are inside of my own skin. I haven't anything to throw away. No one has ever taken a drink who did not honestly believe at the start that he could take it or let it alone as he wished, but their experience shows that they miscalculated the power of their enemy.

"In such contests whiskey is nearly always the victor. Knowing this, I will not gamble on my chances of drinking and remaining my own master. I am my own master now, and I shall retain my mastership. I here assert my manhood, my inherited divinity, the power given me by my Creator, which enables me to conquer this monster drink or any other enemy of my manhood. I believe with Saint Bernard that 'nothing can harm me but myself,' and hereby pledge myself to do nothing that will make me less of a man. I am poised in divine power. I am one with the One."

If any form of vice has gotten a grip upon you, don't let it frighten you or drive you to despair, but brace yourself at once to get rid of it. Remember that there is something within you that never can fall, that never can be stained, – that is the God image. Just say to yourself, "If God made me, then I must partake of God's qualities; I must have power to overcome any evil habit. This cursed thing which is ruining my chances of future success and happiness is an insult to my manhood, an insult to my ideal of womanhood, an insult to my future wife, a crime against my future children. It is not stronger than I am; it is weaker. I will no longer allow it to usurp my power, to smirch my manhood, honeycomb my character and destroy my self-respect. I hereby take a sacred oath with myself never to repeat that which will cover up the divine image in me, lessen my chances in life, ruin my health and make me a failure, the wreck of a man. I am a conqueror, not a slave; a divine force, not a weak, abject thing. I claim my birthright as a son of God. I am a man, strong, successful, happy, and free. 'I am the Captain of my soul.'"

Whether in conquering an enemy habit, driving out fear, or worry, or overcoming trouble or difficulty of any sort, the repetition in our heart-to heart talks of some strong, encouraging, uplifting Bible passages, such as the following, will be found very helpful.

"I the Lord will hold thy right hand, saying unto thee, Fear not; I will help thee." "I will be glad and rejoice in Thy mercy; for Thou hast considered my trouble. Thou hast known my soul in adversities." "The joy of the Lord is your strength." "They that wait upon the Lord shall renew their strength; they shall mount up with wings as eagles." "Whoso putteth his trust in the Lord shall be safe." "I sought the Lord and He heard me and delivered me from all my fears." "Cast thy burden upon the Lord and He shall sustain thee."

If you are a vacillator; if your great weakness is indecision; if you have a horror of being forced to make a prompt decision; if you are inclined to leave everything until the last minute because you cannot bear to close anything of importance, to cut off the possibility of taking it up again for reconsideration; if you leave your letters unsealed, important papers unsigned, contracts open until you are actually forced to close them, for fear you may wish to reconsider your decisions, you can cure yourself of your weakness by talking to your inner self about it, and making up your mind to be a man of decision instead of a vacillator, a weakling.

Resolve every morning that for that day at least you will decide things promptly, that you will act like a man of firm purpose and definite will, one who is characterized by a faculty for vigorous, quick decision. After you have given yourself a reasonable time to look over the matter calling for decision and to reach a conclusion, say to yourself, "This is the course to follow," or "This is the right thing to do. I will decide now and get it off my mind. I will not reconsider, or open the question up again. My judgment is correct. I will trust it. I can think clearly, and decide vigorously, without procrastinating or vacillating, and from this day on I will do so."

Impersonate every day someone you admire for his promptness in putting things through, for his vigorous self-confidence and power of quick and final decision. No matter if you make mistakes at first, stick to your resolve to decide things once for all. When a letter is written let it be sealed and done with. When you have agreed to do a thing, do it at once; burn your bridges behind you and leave no tempting way of retreat in case you wish to reconsider your case. And continually reinforce yourself throughout the day with positive affirmations, – "I am," "I can," "I will."

But remember, if you do not act with the same grim resolution in making good your words as the French soldiers did at Verdun, they will be worse than useless.

Always carry yourself as though you were marching to victory, make this impression upon everyone who sees you. Let victory stand out of your very face, let it speak out of your eyes with such determination, with such vigorous resolution that people will know that there is no such thing as keeping you down, no such thing as discouraging you, because you are victory-organized, because you are in the habit of winning. Give people the suggestion of invincibility. This will be worth more to you than a large amount of money capital without it, or with an appearance of cowardice or defeat in your face, a suggestion of weakness or doubt, fear as to the outcome of your career.

Think what the suggestion of invincibility in a general of an army means! Think what it means to Joffre! The French people know that there is no such thing as defeating him in the end, no such thing as defeating his pluck or his grit. They know that as long as his life shall last courage will be there, will lead the way. They know that his grim resolve will never yield. Think what such an appearance of invincibility would mean to you!

These heart-to-heart talks are merely suggestions, or models of the self-treatment method of overcoming bad habits or defects of character, for acquiring strength and developing the qualities that make for nobility, success, happiness, righteousness. They may be adapted to meet the requirements of different personal needs, and if practiced faithfully every day, several times during the day, if possible, and just before retiring at night, they will, if backed up by earnest effort to make your words true, do wonders in bringing about the desired results.

Talking to yourself may at first seem silly to you, but you will soon get accustomed to it and feel its beneficial effects. You will think more highly of yourself, you will have more self-respect, more self-confidence; you will believe more in yourself, you will have more assurance, more confidence in your ability, you will stand higher in your own estimate in every way. This does not mean that you will become egotistical or conceited, but simply that you will know yourself and your possibilities better, and be able to use to better advantage all the power and talent God has given you.

In your heart-to-heart talks always encourage yourself; always talk up, never down. In every possible way try to establish confidence in yourself, because a great self-faith is a powerful force, a creative force. "According to thy faith be it unto thee." That is, according to the degree, the intensity, the persistency of your faith, so will be your realization.

11
OUR PARTNERSHIP WITH GOD

THE NEARER we are to Omnipotence the greater our strength.

Life will take on new meaning, greater dignity, a higher power when we live in constant realization of our at-one-ment with our Creator, our at-one-ment with the One, our partnership with the All-Good.

When Christ emphasized the fact that the kingdom of Heaven is within us, He meant that this kingdom within is identical with the great cosmic intelligence of the universal mind, and that here we tap the source of all supply. The kingdom that is within us is the kingdom of power. It is in the great within of us that we make wireless connections with Omnipotence, with Omniscience, with Omnipresence. Here is where we actually feel the pulsation of the allness and the everywhereness of God, and are conscious of our connection with the One, our oneness with the All-good.

The greatest discovery of the centuries is the discovery of the identity, the oneness of the mind in our subconscious selves with the great universal mind, the cosmic intelligence.

"What discovery in twenty centuries," says Dr. Abel T. Allen "compares with this, that man has learned to tap the universal mind, the infinite reservoir of his own soul and thereby create health, ability, character, or any other quality he may desire?"

The idea that man can control and adapt to his own growth and enlargement the cosmic intelligence which flows to him through his subconscious self; that by his own power of choice and will this cosmic, creative intelligence everywhere present can be utilized by man as a creative force, is one of the most astounding truths that has ever come to the human mind.

Years ago Henry Ward Beecher said that thinking is creating with God. Yet how few of us realize even today that we cannot think without creating and that if we think helpful thoughts, unselfish thoughts, love thoughts we are creating with God.

The new thought of God takes God into partnership, and when we realize the divine cooperation in our lives we think as "we," not "I."

This new thought of God gives us a new conception of man and of his relation to his God. It teaches us that we are a vital, inseparable part of Deity; that we are a part of the great creative Mind, and that we are creating every day, because we cannot think, we cannot feel, we cannot act without creating something.

The new philosophy of life teaches us that there is something in man that is inviolable, something that was never born and will never die, something that cannot be contaminated, that cannot sin. It teaches us that there is a divinity within us which is never impaired; that no matter what happens to the rest of us, this divinity, the God in us, is untarnished, inviolable.

A human being's power depends very largely upon his God consciousness, upon his conscious partnership with his Creator. The closer the relation, the closer the man's God-consciousness, the consciousness of his oneness with the One, the more power he can express, because he draws upon the limitless resources of his Infinite Partner.

Many people seem to have an idea that the creative intelligence out of which everything we know has been created was, in the beginning, localized somewhere in a Creator's mind, but we now know that this great creative intelligence or force is everywhere. We know that it exists in every cell in our bodies, and in every created object.

Just as the entire man with all the traits and characteristics of his ancestors, and with his own possibilities and his own destiny, was wrapped up in the microscopic protoplasm which unfolds into the full-grown man, so the future lily, the rose, the tree, the fruit, the vegetable, lives in the apparently unorganized protoplasmic germ from which it started. In these microscopic germs creative intelligence dwells. Every atom, every electron in the universe is the home of the divine intelligence which creates and sustains all things.

This intelligence is not fragmentary in the atom or electron, any more than certain parts of the oak are fragmentary in the acorn. The whole of the mighty oak lives in possibility in the acorn. There is nothing added to the oak which was not an amplification of the cell life in the acorn. What the soil, the chemistry of the sun, the moisture and the atmosphere have added to it were mere helps to the unfolding of the germs in the acorn.

What is true of the oak, or any other created thing is true of man. The entire Lincoln lived in the protoplasmic germ from which he sprang. All his possibilities were there. His environment, his education, the part he played in life were merely helps to unfold, to bring out that possible Lincoln which existed in the protoplasmic germ.

The new thought of God shows us that creation has never been finished; that it is a perpetual process which never ceases to be operative. It teaches that the Creator is never separate from His creation, that man is not a separate unit thrown off to sink or swim at the mercy of chance, or a cruel destiny, but that he is one with his Maker, united with Him in creative work. It declares that he is a part of the infinite intelligence, of the universal mind, and that he expresses so much of the great universal intelligence as he can appropriate and utilize.

Anything we ever can need or want is in us awaiting release, awaiting expression. The thought of separateness from our divine Source robs us of power to express or create, because we can only have that degree of power which our consciousness embodies. Only that is ours which we can express. All of our weakness, our troubles, our worries, our fears, our sufferings, and our diseases come from our conscious separation from our living, vital, throbbing, creative force.

We now know that man is like a partner in an enormous concern. His resources are not limited to his own little capital. He can draw upon the firm as long, as there is anything to draw. We are all God's partners, and our capacity for creation depends very largely upon our consciousness of our divine partnership.

"When man discovers his identity with Spirit he begins to manifest Creation on his own account," says one writer. "No longer a passive instrument, tool, or chessman in the cosmic life, he becomes a center of creative power in himself. It is true that he sees the phenomenal world for what it really is; he sees that prizes and rewards of life are mere baubles and trinkets; and he strives no longer for them for themselves.

But, in place of the old illusion, he sees a creative purpose in the cosmic activities, a meaning in the universal 'becoming,' and he smiles and takes his place again on the stage of life, playing his part willingly, cheerfully, confidently, and understandingly. His peep behind the scenes does not interfere with his characterization and the portrayal of his appointed part; on the contrary, he plays his part all the better by reason of his knowing."

When we have taken God into partnership we are conscious that we are God-polarized, that we are in the current which runs God-ward. The consciousness of God, of being reinforced and buttressed with infinite power, supported by infinite wisdom, gives a wonderfully increased sense of power. When you realize your divine partnership, it will enlarge your life and multiply your effectiveness, because it will take away from you all sense of uncertainty, all feeling of inability to buffet the storms of life, all sense of hopelessness in the presence of overwhelming odds. It will give a new meaning to living because you will know that you are not a victim of Fate, but that your life is founded upon infallible fundamental principles.

When you take God into full, complete partnership you will never fear. Your life's venture cannot end in chagrin. You will never suffer lack or want, because you will then know that if you want success, prosperity or anything needful, you must take the material into your mind which will create what you desire. You will head toward your ideals, toward the material which you hold in your mind, and this is the stuff life is made of. You will be led in green pastures and beside the still waters, and you will fear no evil; no pestilence can touch you because you are God-polarized, you are immune from all of the ills of the flesh.

Holding steadily in mind the ideals of the things you want to bring to pass, the ideal of the man you want to be and the things you want to accomplish, is actually necessary to the further process of creating.

Think of the miracles man has wrought by holding his ideal in mind and working in cooperation with his God! Compare, for instance, our fruits and vegetables of today with the same kind of fruits and vegetables as they were before man focused his mind upon improving them and lifting them to higher levels! Compare the luscious Indian River orange today with the sour, gnarled, bitter wild orange, the best that nature, unassisted by man, could give us!

We know, of course, that man alone, without the creative power implanted in him by God, never could have evolved the luscious fruits and succulent vegetables of all sorts which we enjoy today out of the original inferior products as unassisted nature left them.

The marvelous improvements man has made upon the earth in lifting the things which God originally created to higher and higher and ever higher levels can only be accounted for through his co-partnership with his Creator. It is the God in man working with the God in the great cosmic intelligence which has lifted them to such heights.

The work which man has accomplished in a multitude of different ways proves that he is one with God, that he is a co-creator with Him, and that together they can do what neither could do alone. They are working together for the betterment of the race. Without the God power which, consciously or unconsciously, is flowing through him, man could do nothing. Alone he would be powerless; and yet it is a strange thing that some of our greatest inventors and discoverers have been skeptics, unbelievers in God, when it was the God in them that helped them to make their inventions or their discoveries.

As a matter of fact, when a man invents or discovers that which benefits his fellow men, whether he acknowledges it or not, it is because the creative force in him is cooperating with the divine force in the universal intelligence which is everywhere present.

It is the creative force of divinity in Edison that has produced these marvelous inventions and facilities for eliminating drudgery from, and beautifying, life, which Edison and his Maker together have given to the world.

Did you ever stop to think that practically all of the great inventions and discoveries, improvements and facilities which are emancipating human beings from drudgery and hard, painful conditions, and lifting mankind to a higher level, were once regarded as "impossibilities?" Did you ever realize that at one time those who attempted to make these "impossibilities" realities were ridiculed, called cranks or insane? People thought they were obsessed, but they were obsessed only with the divine urge to create. This obsession would not let them rest until they had realized in the actual the model which they had first formed in the mind. Think of the innumerable things man has accomplished, even within the past century, how he has triumphed over the obstacles that to the great majority seemed insuperable, and succeeded by his creative energy in literally bringing the ends of the earth together!

It is the great God force working with and through them that has enabled men in every age to accomplish the "impossible." This force is back of the telephone, back of wireless telegraphy, back of the steamship, the automobile, the airship, back of the moving picture, the phonograph, and every invention that has helped the world along its upward path.

No inventor can take personal credit for the vision which came to him ready made. It is in his personal effort, in his persistent self-sacrificing struggle to make his vision a reality that man's strength and divinity are manifested.

He is the working medium, but still only the medium, through which the electric light power, the telephone, the wireless and all the other marvelous things we are now enjoying came to the world.

Mr. Edison says that he regards himself merely as a channel between the great cosmic intelligence and the race for the passing along of inventions which benefit mankind. Other great benefactors of the race felt as he does. They did not believe that they really originated the wonderful things which they passed along to posterity, but that their minds were particularly adapted to reaching into the great cosmic ocean of intelligence and attracting the things which they gave to the world. They felt, like Edison, that they were mediums for the transmission of special blessings to man.

It is man working with God, the divine force, the God in man working with the great creative divinity that is lifting the race and improving mankind. Man is not doing this as a separate unit.

There is a power in him back of the flesh but not of it, working with the divine intelligence in the great cosmic ocean of thought, of cosmic intelligence. This power is everywhere operative and is destined to lift every created thing up to the heights of its greatest possibility.

This is what is going, above all, to help every man to play his part to the limit of his ability in the great universal drama, to make his highest possible contribution to the universe. This is how the millennium will be brought about, by the cooperation of the divinity in man with the divine intelligence in the cosmic world.

There seems to be no limit to man's possibilities as a miracle worker when he works with his God. The brainiest man that ever lived has never yet exhausted in any one direction the cooperative marvels of his Maker. Who can imagine what our fruits, our flowers, our vegetables, our cereals, our animals, will be after another thousand years of the cooperative effort of man with God!

The chrysanthemum which takes the prize at flower shows today is a miracle of size and beauty compared with the tiny, scrubby chrysanthemum from which it sprang centuries ago. The same thing is true of the rose, the carnation, the pansy, and all garden flowers. At the same rate of improvement who can foretell what these things will develop into even a hundred years from now!

The marvelous creations which Luther Burbank, cooperating with his God, has produced in the kingdom of flowers and plants are but indications of what the future will bring.

"Nature unaided fails" is the dictum of science. Luther Burbank is a partner with his Creator. Together they are doing what neither could do alone.

Man is a necessary instrument in the creative process. The Creator alone never has produced such wonderful things as Burbank and the Creator together have produced. Nor are Burbank, Edison and other noted men exceptions in this respect. We are all co-creators with the great Creator of all.

Man as God's partner is performing miracles all over the world. He mixes his brains with the soil, and behold, what marvelous creations he calls out, as if he had touched it with a magic wand! By his genius in selecting and combining stocks in the animal and the vegetable world, he evolves the perfect plant, the thoroughbred animal. The same mysterious cosmic intelligence that pushes into the inventor's mind the image and the plan of a great invention is helping the horticulturist, the agriculturist, the stock breeder, the scientist, – all who are engaged in creative and productive work.

Every great writer, artist, inventor, – everyone who has done a really great thing, – has felt conscious of receiving suggestions from outside of his own brain, quite apart from what he has received from other sources, – books, people, nature, study, etc. In other words, he is conscious of being helped by some great power back of his brain.

Great writers, for example, do not deliberately think out in detail the things they are going to write. Pictures come to them, ideas flood their brains. Sometimes with such an onrush do ideas come that they cannot write them all down or even dictate them. In moments of inspiration like this the poet, the author, the musician, is merely a sort of secretary for the mysterious intelligence back of his brain.

Call it what we will, divine force or the cosmic intelligence, that exists back of all atoms, in all electrons, there is certainly a formative intelligence that plans, and makes the creative artist feel that he is merely the wireless receiving station taking off an immortal message, a message that has been flashed from a divine station somewhere in the universe.

How often have messages been transmitted to the inventor during sleep, when he has been totally unconscious of trying to think or plan an invention! How often has the poet received in a dream, as by a flash of illumination, the line or the words he needed to complete a poetic image!

Whence come these things? What formed that divine image which lives first in the artist's brain? He did not deliberately plan that picture which came to him full-orbed, perfect! His own brain did not fashion the ideal. He merely reproduced it on canvas.

Whence came that model in the sculptor's brain, which his imagination holds until with chisel and mallet and deft hand he calls it out of the marble in a wonderful statue that all but breathes and lives. The sculptor did not deliberately make his mental model. It came to him. He used it to help him call his idea out of the block of marble. Without it there would be no statue.

There is no other explanation than that it came to him through the great creative Mind. All of these things go to show that man and God are one, that they are working together, that they are partners, co-creators, that everywhere they cooperate in producing, creating, improving, uplifting.

No one is a real success until he takes God (Good) into partnership, until his own purpose and ambition are squared with the divine plan. That is, a man's vocation must at least not run counter to the purpose of the universe, which is based on the unity of all things, which means team work.

If you are doing things which in some way benefit the race, contribute to its highest welfare, then your career is in tune with the Infinite plan.

You are cooperating with the Creator in the team work of the race. You are a success. But if you are doing something which runs counter to God's world plan, to this great cooperative team work of the race, you are a failure, and you cannot be really happy, because you are working in opposition to your Creator.

There is something inside of a man which protests against doing that which tends to injure another, that which does not square with his God nature, with the best thing in him; that which is not working in response to his highest aspiration.

This is why men who are in questionable vocations never feel quite right about their work. They are never proud of it. Their hearts are not in it. They would rather strangers would not know what they are doing, unless they see in them the marks of the brute, those things which have an affinity for their own animality.

I have met professional gamblers, liquor dealers, bar tenders, dive keepers, and I have never known one who did not really feel ashamed to have decent people know how they got their living.

When a man is selling useful merchandise, working as a section hand on a railroad, as a street cleaner, as a day laborer in any useful field, he is not ashamed of his work – unless, through lack of ambition or for any other reason he is doing the lower thing when something very much higher is possible to him. But, no matter how humble, needful service, work which helps the race along, is dignified, and, if done in the right spirit, will be an opening to something higher.

When you take God into partnership, when you are conscious that you are doing His work, you have a feeling of peace and security. You walk as one who sees a great light because you feel that you have a great Partner, One with whom you cannot lose your way. You do not fear failure because you know that your divine Partner is the very Source of all supply, and you feel safe, reassured. You know that nothing can prevent your success as long as you and your Partner are in harmony.

Taking God into partnership means that you must not only be honest, but that you must be robustly honest. You know that you cannot lie or cheat or steal. You know that you cannot take advantage of anybody.

You know that you must be kind and considerate to all. You know that you cannot be greedy or grasping, and at the same time work with God.

If you take God into partnership you know that you must be clean and pure-minded. You know that you cannot indulge in low, sensual pleasures. You know you cannot do anything which will degrade another or push further down one who is already on the downgrade. Your plea that that one is already bad is no excuse for you. If you take God into partnership you cannot despoil or desecrate His creature. She is your sister. You cannot take advantage of God's child and have God for a partner, because you will then be working against Him instead of with Him.

Thousands of young men start with God as a partner and lose Him because He will not do business with a man who is not clean, pure, and honest. If you would keep God as a partner you must do right and be right.

"I am the life and substance of the Greater' Mind," says Paul Ellsworth, "and the recognition of this truth frees me from every false desire." When you realize that you are one with the Greater Mind, you will naturally take God into partnership, and work in perfect harmony with Him. This will give a new meaning to your life, and will turn you around completely so that you will see the things that are really worthwhile. You will see a new world. You will have a new zest in life, a new ambition, an ambition for the attainment of the higher things, the things that give enduring satisfaction. You will lose interest in that which before you thought essential, imperative, to your happiness.

The things you drop will not be wrenched away from you. You will drop them voluntarily for something better, just as the child will drop the apple for the orange, the orange for the toy, and the toy in turn for something better, something bigger and more attractive. Your motto will then be, "The best of everything belongs to me because I am working in harmony with the Creator and inherit the best from the King of kings."

When we have a Partner who is the reality of wisdom, of love, of justice, a Partner who is the very source of all supply, we do not fear want, we do not fear poverty, we do not fear sickness or death. We fear nothing because we know we are united with Omnipotent Power, and that nothing but ourselves can sever this divine connection.

Made in the USA
Lexington, KY
05 March 2016